"A brilliant map for the real an[...] This is medicine we need right [...]

America's Racial Karma: An [...]

"Kaira Jewel Lingo is one of the most authentic Dharma teachers of our generation. Her decades of committed and genuine practice have yielded a book that speaks to what so many of us are longing for—a path of guidance through some of the most difficult experiences of our lives. *We Were Made for These Times* is nothing but needed medicine during this time of needed healing."
—LAMA ROD OWENS, author of *Love and Rage: The Path of Liberation through Anger*

"Times of darkness hold the power and potential for deep transformation. Kaira Jewel Lingo is a wise and inspiring guide in navigating the challenges of our times with courage, equanimity, and compassion. She shares timeless teachings and practices that reveal our belonging and free our hearts." —TARA BRACH, author of *Trusting the Gold: Uncovering Your Natural Goodness*

"A treasure trove of loving and practical meditation advice about how we can navigate through difficult times and challenging transitions with our heart and mind intact....One of the best commentaries I have seen on the everyday usefulness of Thich Nhat Hanh's life of teachings, this book is uniquely tailored to our times. A gem of a work!" —JAN WILLIS, author of *Dreaming Me: Black, Baptist, and Buddhist*

"A most beautiful weaving of the many Wisdom threads in Buddhist practice to create a sacred mantle of Freedom for us all."
—LARRY YANG, author of *Awakening Together: The Spiritual Practice of Inclusivity and Community*

"I love this book! Simple yet profound, heartfelt and insightful, far-reaching and practical. Kaira Jewel Lingo draws on her years as a nun with Thich Nhat Hanh to offer the ideas, tools, and experiential practices we need to weather topsy-turvy times. A true gem." —RICK HANSON, PhD, author of *Neurodharma*

"From a jewel of a teacher, a simple and clear way to access your own heart and wisdom.... Anyone seeking answers will find relief in the pages of this book." —ZENJU EARTHLYN MANUEL, author of *The Deepest Peace*

"*We Were Made for These Times* reads like a poem. Kaira Jewel Lingo offers inspiring and accessible guidance for experiencing the nearness of freedom despite our circumstances. A timely and timeless read for all." —RUTH KING, author of *Mindful of Race*

"This hopeful book brings light to our times so darkened by the shadows of ecocide, racism, patriarchy, illusion, and despair. Kaira Jewel Lingo's story alone offers great hope, for it demonstrates how a new generation is rising."
—MATTHEW FOX, author of *Original Blessing*

"A beautiful book, written from a place of deep love and wisdom. The author's depth of understanding, born of many years of practice, is conveyed with exceptional grace and simplicity, and her invitation to join together on this path of peace and freedom is irresistible."
—JOSEPH GOLDSTEIN, author of *Mindfulness*

"Kaira Jewel Lingo is a true teacher."
—SATISH KUMAR, founder of Schumacher College and *Resurgence & Ecologist* magazine

WE WERE
MADE FOR
THESE TIMES

WE WERE MADE
FOR THESE
TIMES

*Ten Lessons on Moving
through Change, Loss, and
Disruption*

Kaira Jewel Lingo

PARALLAX PRESS
BERKELEY, CALIFORNIA

Parallax Press

2236 B Sixth Street

Berkeley, California 94710

parallax.org

Parallax Press is the publishing division of
Plum Village Community of Engaged Buddhism

Cover art by Edmund Weiss, *Leonid Meteor Storm*, 1833

Cover design by Katie Eberle

Text design by Zoe Norvell

Author photo © Kaira Jewel Lingo

Plum Village songs from *A Basket of Plums* by Thich Nhat Hanh and
Joseph Emet reprinted courtesy of Parallax Press and the Plum Village
Community of Engaged Buddhism.

Printed on recycled paper in the United States of America

Library of Congress Cataloging-in-Publication Data

Names: Lingo, Kaira Jewel, author.

Title: We were made for these times : ten lessons on moving through
change, loss, and disruption / Kaira Jewel Lingo.

Description: Berkeley, California : Parallax Press, 2021 |
Includes bibliographical references.

Identifiers: LCCN 2021031195 (print) | LCCN 2021031196 (ebook) |
ISBN 9781946764928 (trade paperback) | ISBN 9781952692208 (ebook)

Subjects: LCSH: Self-actualization (Psychology) | Peace of mind. |
Meditation. | Calmness.

Classification: LCC BF637.S4 L5637 2021 (print) | LCC BF637.S4 (ebook)
| DDC 158.1—dc23

LC record available at https://lccn.loc.gov/2021031195

LC ebook record available at https://lccn.loc.gov/2021031196

2 3 4 5 / 25 24 23 22

To those seeking to find their way
and to all those in the chrysalis

Some periods of our growth are so confusing that we don't even recognize that growth is happening. We may feel hostile or angry or weepy and hysterical, or we may feel depressed. It would never occur to us, unless we stumbled on a book or a person who explained to us, that we were in fact in the process of change, of actually becoming larger, spiritually, than we were before. Whenever we grow, we tend to feel it, as a young seed must feel the weight and inertia of the earth as it seeks to break out of its shell on its way to becoming a plant. Often the feeling is anything but pleasant. But what is most unpleasant is the not knowing what is happening. Those long periods when something inside ourselves seems to be waiting, holding its breath, unsure about what the next step should be, eventually become the periods we wait for, for it is in those periods that we realize that we are being prepared for the next phase of our life and that, in all probability, a new level of the personality is about to be revealed.

—Alice Walker,
Living by the Word

Grant that I may be given appropriate difficulties and sufferings on this journey so that my heart may be truly awakened and my practice of liberation and universal compassion may be truly fulfilled.

—Tibetan Buddhist prayer
quoted by Jack Kornfield in
A Path with Heart

CONTENTS

PREFACE

This is the era of just redemption
we feared at its inception
We did not feel prepared to be the heirs
of such a terrifying hour
but within it we found the power
to author a new chapter.
To offer hope and laughter to ourselves.
So while once we asked,
how could we possibly prevail over catastrophe?
Now we assert,
How could catastrophe possibly prevail over us?

—Amanda Gorman,
"The Hill We Climb"[1]

I warmly welcome you on this journey of learning how we can move through times of transition and challenge with clarity and compassion.[2] I have found the practice of staying present, openhearted, and accepting of changing life circumstances to be incredibly helpful through my own major life transitions and challenges. Two of the most significant transitions have been becoming a Buddhist nun at age twenty-five and then leaving monastic life fifteen years later.

I grew up in an interracial family within an ecumenical Christian order that developed a new kind of monasticism for families focused on voluntary simplicity and service to the poor and marginalized. I was raised in a residential community in Chicago of several hundred people and several thousand globally, with spiritual practice at the heart of our collective life. I remember, as a child, waking up to a bell at 5:30 a.m. each day and then going to daily office for prayer at 6:00 a.m. Starting from the age of eight, I spent four rich and impactful years in an area considered "one of Africa's biggest slums" on the outskirts of Nairobi while my dad was engaged in our religious community's work of village development in Kenya and other East African countries.

As a child in Kenya, I fed my passion for dance with rigorous ballet lessons and also was grateful to learn horse riding. Because I loved Spanish, I spent a summer in Mexico when I turned fifteen, and my experience of racism and discrimination in the United States led me to spend a year as an exchange student in Brazil so I could taste living in a country with a more fluid relationship to race, one that offered a powerful experience of the African diaspora. That is where I began playing capoeira, the Afro-Brazilian martial art that I continued to study through my early twenties, writing my bachelor's and master's thesis on this African-inspired art. I was a serious student and enjoyed school, went to Stanford, and spent my junior year at Howard University so I could relish the experience of being at one of America's famed historically Black universities and embrace my own experience of being Black. I had thick, curly hair, wore colorful, batik clothes, and experienced a deeply nurturing and mutually loving relationship in my last two years of college. I was also a keen spiritual seeker and had begun exploring spirituality through meditation and yoga.

Yet, as I was finishing my master's degree, I felt that there was something missing from my education. Ram Dass once gave a talk on the Stanford campus and said, "You learn a lot of things here, but you don't learn how to be happy." I knew that in spite of all the wonderful things I had learned, I still needed to learn to be happy and to take care of my suffering. So, I set out traveling to find a spiritual teacher and community where I could learn how to be at ease with myself, and not just academically successful. At age twenty-three, in Plum Village, France, I knew I had met my teacher as soon as I saw the Vietnamese Zen master Thich Nhat Hanh. The simplicity and grace with which he taught and practiced mindfulness was so compelling that I cancelled the rest of my four-month trip around Europe to continue practicing in the monastery, and at the end of that time, I had the wish to become a nun. I thought, *Why not do what is most important for me now?* I figured we never know how long we have to live, so I wanted to prioritize what I cared about most.

I became a Buddhist nun at age twenty-five in the community of Thich Nhat Hanh, whom his students call *Thay*, or "teacher" in Vietnamese (and I will be referring to him as *Thay* for the rest of the book).

When I ordained, I gave away all my material possessions, shaved my head, wore simple robes, and practiced celibacy. I moved from a large city in the United States to the rural countryside of France. I was now living with hundreds of monks and nuns, the majority of whom were of Vietnamese origin but also came from all over the globe. For fifteen years I lived in monasteries on several continents and traveled extensively in the US, Asia, Africa, and Latin America, teaching and practicing mindfulness.

Then, in my early forties, after spending nearly my whole adult life as a nun, I made another huge shift, deciding to leave monastic life to start all over. So, when many friends from my youth had already started families and spent several decades in their professions, I was learning in middle age to do the things my peers had been doing since their early twenties—paying taxes, using a cell phone, running a household, and online dating! It was a major transition on many levels: personally, socially, financially, professionally, spiritually, and culturally. In a sense, I was reinventing my whole identity.

Whether the challenges or transitions we're facing are desired or not, they can be stressful or destabilizing. Losing a job, feeling a sense of isolation and loneliness, and grieving the passing of a loved one are undoubtedly difficult for everyone. Even joyful events such as welcoming a new baby into the world, starting a new job, or falling in love may be very disruptive. We are beginning a new chapter of our life and the future is uncertain.

Our personal challenges are not disconnected from the larger challenges and disruptions our world is facing right now. We cannot separate ourselves and be unaffected by the climate emergency, global health threats, growing income inequality, glaring racial wounds, and systemic white supremacy. In this book, we'll learn ways of finding freedom and stability right in the midst of all of this, so that we can meet whatever life brings us with an open heart, a balanced mind, and committed action. We will develop presence, courage, and resilience, the essential qualities for navigating a viable future as individuals and as a species.

I look forward to journeying with you.

Chapter 1

COMING HOME

But the stone that the builder refuse
Shall be the head cornerstone,
And no matter what game they play,
Eh, we got something they could never take away;
We got something they could never take away

> —Bob Marley,
> "Natty Dread Rides Again"

You already are what you want to become.

> —Master Lin Chi

All of us go through times of transition, challenges, and difficulties. We may have faced or will face times of loss, confusion, or heartbreak, when we realize we cannot control the way our life is unfolding, whether in our personal lives or in the world around us. With mindfulness, we can learn to move through these intense, challenging times in ways that don't add to the suffering and difficulty that are already there. We can even learn to open our hearts to the richness and wisdom these times of immense disruption can bring us.

A key step that can help us begin to settle ourselves when we are profoundly unsettled is to come home, to ourselves, in this moment, whatever is happening. This is one way of speaking about mindfulness, or being present: *coming home to ourselves.* When we bring our mind back to our body we come home. We could consider this state as *our true home.* This home inside of us is a home no one can take away from us, and it cannot be damaged or destroyed. No matter what happens around us, if we can find this home inside of us, we are always safe.

When we touch this experience of coming home, it is like we have finally arrived home after a long journey. We experience a sense of peace and even freedom, no matter how confining the outer circumstances. Coming home to ourselves feels like belonging; it is a state that holds us and enables us to hold others.

This is so important because we can live our whole lives estranged from this home within ourselves.

My teacher Thay sums up his whole lifetime of teachings with one sentence: "I have arrived, I am home." For him, the principal aim of mindfulness practice is to experience that we have *already arrived*, here and now. There is nowhere we need to run to or be, other than right here in the present moment. And we experience ourselves at home, no longer looking for some refuge outside of us, in some other place or time, when we touch the truth that all that we long for and search after is here inside of us.

We can experience encountering this spacious and free place of our true home in unexpected moments as we spend more time tuning in to what is happening inside us and around us.

One morning when I was a novice nun, in slow walking after sitting meditation, I became very present and aware of every step. I began by being aware that as I was stepping with my left foot, I was at the same time stepping with my right, because my left foot could not be without my right. And vice versa. Then I saw that my arms were also contained in my feet, so I was also stepping with my arms. Then my hands, my stomach, brain, sense organs, heart, lungs. I was 100 percent with my body. I was tasting the earth with my feet, listening to it, looking at it, feeling it, knowing it, smelling it with my feet. My heart was loving it, my lungs breathing it in and out.

Then I turned my attention more towards the Earth and knew I was also walking on cool streams of water flowing under me, and hot, fiery liquid deep below, in the center of the Earth. I imagined walking on the feet of those directly opposite us on the other side of the planet. The soles of my feet touched the soles of a little baby taking tentative steps, and a pregnant woman, and an old grandpa. My feet touched the feet of a lonely isolated person, and someone carried away by hatred and anger. I was also walking on the feet of someone who was right then doing walking meditation and enjoying the present moment. I was one with those walking the Earth whose hearts were filled with love and peace.

If we're not aware of what is happening in the moment because we are caught up in our thoughts or reveries, or in the grip of worry or other strong emotions, it's as if we have left our house. If we stay away for a long time, dust accumulates and unwanted visitors may take up residence in our home. Things like stress and tension accumulate in our bodies and minds, and over time, if we don't tend to them, they can lead to physical or psychological illness.

But the beauty of awareness is that we can always return home to ourselves. Our home is always there, waiting for us to come back. There are numerous ways we can go home to ourselves: by being aware of our breath, by being aware of body sensations or bodily movements, and by connecting with the reality around us, like the sounds in our environment. And when we come back home in these ways, we are able to take stock and survey the territory of our being, seeing clearly what parts of our inner landscape need more support, where we need to pay more attention.

It is especially tempting in times of transition and challenge to abandon our homes, to leave our territory, in search of answers, perhaps by worrying about what will happen in the future. This is precisely the moment when we need to return to the present moment, feel our bodies, and take good care of ourselves now. Because *the future is made of this moment.* If we take good care of this moment, even if it is very difficult, we are taking good care of the future.

It may also be hard to come home if we sense that unresolved pain has accumulated and we don't want to face it. We may get into the habit of avoiding our home completely. We don't want to be with those raw, unprocessed parts of our experience that are painful and may be quite scary.

If this is our situation, it is important to have compassion for ourselves for not wanting to return home to face these difficulties inside of us. And yet the only way we can heal them, move through them, and make our home a more cozy place is to turn towards them. As the teaching goes: "The only way out is in." Or through. The practices we will learn in this book will help us to have the courage to go back and put our house in order, and give us the tools to do so, so we can slowly learn to enjoy being back in our true home.

How do we do this? One of the ways is to stay with what is here and now, on the platform of the train station so to speak, watching the trains of our thoughts and plans come and go, rather than jumping on a thought-train that is heading into the future, or another thought-train that takes us into the past. Those plans, worries, and anxieties will surely arise in our mind but we can learn to notice them and take good care of them rather than get carried away by them. Bringing our attention to our breath or to the sensations in our body helps us to stay on the platform of the now. The past and future are not the place where we can come home to ourselves and resource ourselves with the elements we need to move through our difficulties. We can only come home to ourselves in the present moment, in the here and now.

We can spend lots of our time and energy trying to predict or control what the future will bring. This doesn't usually serve us. In truth, we don't need to know what the future will bring. We just need to be right in this moment, and if we touch it deeply, mind and body united, we will find we have all that we need to meet the present. We can't find what we need to meet tomorrow or a month from now because we can't control or exactly know the future, but we will find what we need for right now.

MEDITATION

Coming Home

Let's practice connecting with our present moment experience. Sit, lie, or stand in a comfortable position that supports you to be alert and also relaxed. In the beginning, you may like to hold this book gently in your hands and read the guided meditations, but soon you will be able to start meditating without the book. (You can also listen to the guided meditations on the companion course to this book on Insight Timer, titled "We Were Made for These Times.")[3] You may like to set a timer with your phone or an alarm clock for ten minutes if you wish to be aware of time. Most of these meditations are short, and you can practice them throughout your day.

You are welcome to have your eyes open or closed, and if you keep your eyes open you can choose a spot a few feet in front of you to gaze at softly. Throughout the meditations in this book, wherever you see the ellipses "…" you can pause and allow yourself a few moments to quietly experience the instructions given.

Begin by feeling the contact between your body and whatever surface is supporting you. Let yourself rest in this place, returning to this moment, here and now. Invite whatever parts of yourself that may still be dispersed to come back and settle.

. . .

Allow yourself to settle right here in your body and notice what is here. Is there tension, relaxation, some pain, some pleasure, or a neutral feeling? … As much as you can, bring an attitude of openness to whatever you encounter, without judging your experience. … Whenever you're aware that your mind is distracted in thinking, gently bring it back to your body, to what is right here.

. . .

Set the intention to come home to yourself, to be present for yourself. You deserve this care, you are precious and unique, in all the world there is no one else who brings the precise combination of gifts that you bring. … Allow yourself to arrive here as fully as you can. And welcome the many parts of yourself home.

. . .

You may already begin to feel yourself settling into the home inside of you: the place of your strength, wisdom, and clarity. A place that is trustworthy and capable of providing you with refuge in the storm. But if not, continue to stay with awareness of your body sensations, sounds, or breathing. A sense of coming home will develop over time. It may not happen the first time you meditate, but as you become more attuned to yourself, you will find you have been at home all along.

. . .

If it's helpful, you can repeat inwardly:

I have arrived. I am home.
If it supports you, you can connect the words with your breathing:

Arrived, with the in-breath.
Home, with the out-breath.

. . .

Arrived in the present moment, home in myself, just as I am.

Arrived, arrived,
at home, I am at home,
dwelling in the here and dwelling in the now.
Solid as a mountain, free as a white cloud,
the door to no birth and no death is open,
free and unshakeable.

—Plum Village song[*]

When your timer bell sounds, you can slowly look around your space and gently stretch your limbs.

In Daily Life

You may want to try this practice as you go about your daily life as well, not just in meditation. As you drink your tea, sit in traffic, or wait in line, you can practice coming home to connect with your experience in the moment and arrive in your true home, saying to yourself, "I have arrived, I am home." Remembering that the address of your true home is right here and now.

ooooo

In this first chapter we have explored the way mindfulness can help us come home to ourselves in times of challenge and transition, and how this home is always available to us. We have practiced to experience the

[*]You can hear the songs in this book on the Plum Village website under "Music." Listen to "Arrived" at https://plumvillage.org/articles/arrived/.

home inside of us by being present for ourselves and our body sensations, no matter what they are. We have begun to touch a sense of refuge inside of us.

JOURNALING EXERCISE

What has been your experience
of your true home?

How do you find your way there?

What was helpful in finding your true home?

What support would you need to visit your true
home on a regular basis?

Chapter 2

RESTING BACK AND TRUSTING THE UNKNOWN

When a cat falls out of a tree, it lets go of itself. The cat becomes completely relaxed, and lands lightly on the ground. But if a cat were about to fall out of a tree and suddenly make up its mind that it didn't want to fall, it would become tense and rigid, and would be just a bag of broken bones upon landing.

[I]t is the philosophy of the Tao that … the moment we were born we were kicked off a precipice and we are falling, and there is nothing that can stop it.
So instead of living in a state of chronic tension, and clinging to all sorts of things that are actually falling with us because the whole world is impermanent, be like a cat.

—Alan Watts,
What Is Tao?

Do you have the patience to wait
till your mud settles and the water is clear?
Can you remain unmoving
till the right action arises by itself?

—Lao Tzu

During my fifteen years as a nun, I often heard people ask Thay what to do when facing big life decisions, like which career path to take, whether to separate or stay with their partner, or whether to ordain as a monastic. Thay would often say, "Don't try to figure out the answer by thinking about it." In thinking over a question again and again, we do not generally arrive at real wisdom, but we easily tire ourselves out and get even more confused or anxious.

These deeper life questions can't be resolved at the level of the mind, but must be entrusted to a different, deeper part of our consciousness. Thay suggests we consider this big question as a seed, plant it in the soil of our mind, and let it rest there. Our mindfulness practice in our daily lives is the sunshine and water that the seed needs to sprout so that one day it will rise up on its own, in its own time. And then we'll know the answer to our question without a doubt.

But we must leave the seed down in the soil of our mind and not keep digging it up to see if it is growing roots. It won't grow that way! It is the same with a deep and troubling question. We ask our deeper consciousness to take care of it, and let go of our thinking and worrying about it. Then in our daily lives we practice calming, resting, and coming home to ourselves in the present moment, and that will help the seed of our question to ripen naturally and authentically. This process cannot be rushed or forced. It may take weeks, months, or years. But we can trust that the seed is "down there," being tended to by our deeper consciousness, and one day it will sprout into a clear answer.

In Buddhist psychology this part of our mind is called *store consciousness*. It has the function of storing our memories and all the various mind states we can experience in latent, sleeping form. (I will share more about this in Chapter 5.) For example, maybe you've experienced trying to solve a problem or find an answer to something that perplexes you. You think hard and circle round and round in your mind, but you feel you don't get anywhere. Then you let the question go, and suddenly when you least expect it, inspiration or helpful ideas come to you in a time of rest, and you just know what to do. That is store consciousness operating. It is working on the problem for you while your day-to-day consciousness rests. Store consciousness works in a very natural and easeful way and is much more efficient than our thinking mind. When wisdom arises from store consciousness, it feels right in the body and we no longer have doubts.

But waiting for the answer to arise can be challenging at times because we may really want to know the answer. We may find ourselves feeling deeply insecure and fearful if we don't know what to do, which path to choose. We worry we will make the wrong choice and we catastrophize about what will happen if we take this or that direction. It's hard to find our way if we continue to feed this worry and fear. We can recognize that we are not helping the situation and stop. Returning to this moment, anchoring ourselves in our body, we will find the solidity of the home inside of us, which is capable of helping us find our way, if only we let it, and if we can let go of trying to figure out the future in our heads.

Some years ago, I was trying to discern whether or not to leave the monastic life after having lived as a nun from age twenty-five to forty. During that time, for several years in a row I attended silent retreats at the Insight Meditation Society, or IMS, in Massachusetts. These retreats were six weeks or three months long, and during that whole time, I remained on the retreat grounds, not engaging in the world but coming home to myself. The first meditation began in the hall at 5:00 a.m. and after that was an alternating rhythm of thirty-minute to hour-long periods of sitting and walking meditation, punctuated by a work period, instruction from the teaching team, and delicious meals—including the mouthwatering scent of fresh bread at dinner. The only times of the day I was not in a formal practice period were a short break after lunch and an hour-long fast walk through the woods or on a three-mile loop on backcountry roads that always included some reflective moments by a calm lake. Being in silence, with almost no social interaction except a short meeting with a teacher every few days, gave me the space and time to become closer with myself as there were no other distractions. It was an important experience of pausing to look deeply, and letting my consciousness take its time to find the way.

When I decided to ordain as a nun, in my heart I was making a lifelong commitment. So, it was painful and confusing to find myself questioning this vow that I had assumed would carry me through my entire life. In that time of transition, I didn't know who I was anymore and had no idea who I might become. I was in the midst of a process, like the caterpillar that must dissolve itself completely in the chrysalis to become a butterfly. It was terrifying and extremely uncomfortable when I wanted answers and clarity, when I was used to knowing who I was and where I was going.

Joseph Goldstein was one of my interview teachers on these retreats at IMS. When I shared how distressing it was to find myself with no solid ground under me whatsoever, he mentioned Alan Watts's book *The Wisdom of Insecurity*.[4] It points out that when we are clear and sure about what we are doing, we are less open to the many other possibilities available. But when we let ourselves hang out in the space of not-knowing, there is enormous potential and life could unfold in innumerable ways. So, rather than avoid and fear this place of uncertainty, we can embrace it and all its gifts.

What I found on these long silent retreats was not an answer to my dilemma of whether to leave monastic life or continue as a nun, but rather the ability to dwell more and more comfortably in the experience of not-knowing. I learned to allow the seed of my question to rest in the deeper layers of my consciousness. I was able to touch peace, joy, and well-being in the midst of not-knowing, in the midst of awkwardness and confusion. I learned to let go of fear and resistance right in the midst of dissolving and losing my identity.

By slowing down, choosing to rest back into the uncertainty rather than fighting it, I was able to touch into a sense of space, precisely in moments when it felt like there was no way to keep going and I would be totally overwhelmed. If we can breathe in and out, putting our mind completely on our breathing, or feel our bodies and put all of our attention on the sensations in the body, we can create that space. We slow things down and let our nervous system recalibrate and center. The external situation may not change, but we've changed in relation to our external situation. If we can stop, we have the chance to touch into something deeper than overwhelm. This practice of pausing, or stopping, helps the seed of our question to mature and ripen into the guidance and direction we need.

In a sense, our culture, our society is dissolving. We are collectively entering the chrysalis, and structures we have come to rely on and identify with are breaking down. We are in the cocoon and we don't know what the next phase will be like. Learning to surrender to the unknown in our own lives is essential to our collective learning to move through this time of faster and faster change, disruption, and breakdown.

MEDITATION

Resting Back and Trusting the Unknown

To begin the practice, find a comfortable position, sitting, standing, or lying. Connect with your body and how it's making contact with the chair or the floor. Allow yourself to rest back in some way and really feel the support of whatever is holding you. ... Every time you breathe out, let your body rest even more into the support of the Earth.

. . .

Allow your face to soften, releasing the forehead, the muscles around the eyes, the jaw...

Let the tongue rest in the mouth ...

Be aware of the shoulders and as you breathe out, let the shoulders soften ...

Bring attention to the chest and belly, allow them to release and soften on the next exhale ...

Notice your arms and hands, with the next exhale let them grow a little heavier, releasing tension ...

Feel your legs and feet, as you exhale release, soften, and let go ...

Feel your whole body now as you inhale and exhale, allowing the whole body to soften and release its weight even more onto the Earth ...

. . .

Now bring to mind some question or challenge you may have right now... notice how you feel about it, and the pull that may be there to resolve it ... without trying to figure out an answer or a solution, see this question or challenge as a seed you are entrusting to the soil of your mind, down in its depths ... just allow it to lie there, peacefully, quietly ... let yourself rest back into the unknown, inviting your body to just slightly, actually lean back a tiny bit ... let yourself reconnect with the feeling of being held by the Earth ... you can rest on the Earth, just as this question can rest in the depths of your being ... while it may be scary not to know, there is also infinite possibility here ... take a few deep breaths ... feel your body, settling, present ... and give the seed permission to take the time it needs to ripen into an answer ... trust your own consciousness to show you the way when the time is right.

You may like to practice mindful breathing with the following words:

> *The Buddha* is in me*
> *I have confidence*

And if it's helpful, you are welcome to practice it along with your breathing:

---

*You are welcome to substitute "wisdom and compassion" or "the Christ" or some other sacred word or name for "the Buddha" in this practice.

> *Breathing in, the Buddha is in me,*
> *Breathing out, I have confidence*

It means the capacity of awakening is your nature. You can trust in this.

Let yourself breathe and open to this truth of your own ability to access presence, wisdom, patience, ease, even in the midst of uncertainty. You can do this.

> *Trust, resilience, wisdom is my nature,*
> *I have confidence.*

. . .

> *I entrust myself, I entrust myself, to the Earth, to the Earth, and she entrusts herself to me.*
> —Plum Village song

In Daily Life

You can bring this quality of resting back into your daily life. When you notice yourself leaning into the future, tensing up, trying to predict what will happen, straining to figure out what to do, whether on your own or with others, see if you can actually *physically* rest back. Open up the front of your chest, let your arms hang by your sides, and lean backwards slightly. This can support your mind to rest back, release, and let be, even for a short moment and to whatever degree you are able.

ooooo

In this second chapter we have looked at how we can allow our deep life questions or challenges to rest like a seed in the soil of our mind; we can nurture the seed through daily mindfulness practice, trusting that when it is ready it will sprout on its own and we will know what to do to resolve our question or difficulty.

JOURNALING EXERCISE

Is there a significant life question you have in your mind-heart that you are trying to resolve?

How might you let go of thinking about it so that your deeper consciousness can take care of it for you and lead you to an insight about it?

Can you trust that the answer will come and that you have what you need for the seed to sprout?

Chapter 3

ACCEPTING WHAT IS

When I was a novice, I could not understand why, if
the world is filled with suffering, the Buddha has
such a beautiful smile. Why isn't he disturbed by all
the suffering? Later I discovered that the Buddha has
enough understanding, calm, and strength; that is why
the suffering does not overwhelm him. He is able to
smile to suffering because he knows how to take care of
it and to help transform it. We need to be aware of the
suffering, but retain our clarity, calmness, and strength
so we can help transform the situation. The ocean of
tears cannot drown us if *karuna* [compassion] is there.
That is why the Buddha's smile is possible.

—Thich Nhat Hanh,
Teachings on Love

One of the things that can make navigating times
of transition and challenge even more difficult is
when we resist the changes coming at us or we think
there's something wrong with our life, or with us, when
the road gets bumpy. We may believe that life is not
supposed to be this way. That if we plan and prepare
carefully enough, or act in a meticulously organized fash-
ion, or follow all the rules, we can stay in control and our
life circumstances will remain smooth and predictable.

But transition and challenge are a part of life. They are not wrong or bad. In the Buddha's most essential teaching of the Four Noble Truths, he shares his discovery that suffering is a part of life, and there is no escape from it. This is the first Noble Truth and acknowledging it can help us to suffer less. If we can accept where we are, and not judge the disruption in our life as wrong or bad, we can touch great freedom. This is because fighting what is actually doesn't work. As the saying goes, "Whatever we resist persists."

In *The Heart of the Buddha's Teaching*, Thich Nhat Hanh writes, "We need suffering in order to see the path. … If we are afraid to touch our suffering, we will not be able to realize the path of peace, joy, and liberation. Don't run away. Touch your suffering and embrace it. Make peace with it."

I love the US-based TV show *This Is Us*. In an episode in Season 4, the character Rebecca Pearson, the matriarch of the family, decides to embrace her recent diagnosis of Alzheimer's, to stop fearing or worrying about what she will lose, and to live her life as deeply as possible while it's still available to her. She makes peace with the tragedy of her illness and decides to enjoy the time still left to her.

Thay often said, "A true practitioner isn't someone who doesn't suffer, but someone who knows how to handle their suffering." We could say that the measure of our accomplishment or success is not that our life has no ups and downs, but that we can surf the waves!

I first ordained as a novice nun in 1999. I had been living in Plum Village for a year with the other lay-women and I had my space, my freedom. Somehow, I expected that when I ordained, I would become this angelic, totally peaceful, and happy nun. But when I became a nun, I began living with the sisters in their more crowded quarters. There was one sister I felt uncomfortable with, and now I couldn't avoid her. I would meet her in the bathroom, in the common room, in the dining room. And suddenly I realized I was suffering more and experiencing more anger than when I was a layperson. I thought it would be just the opposite! At first, I resisted this new development, thinking that something was wrong with me. But after a while I realized this was exactly why I ordained, for these difficult emotions to arise so I could see them clearly and learn how to take care of them. If they didn't arise, I wouldn't be able to work with them and trans-form them. The picture of monastic life as free of all pain was quickly replaced by the reality of a life that was going to give me ample opportunity to be a good mindfulness practitioner—not by avoiding my suffering, but by learning to take good care of it.

I have found the same to be true in my new life after the monastery. A loving and committed relationship, a comfortable and beautiful home, and a fulfilling and meaningful vocation are things I am immensely grateful for and yet they are not an escape from all that needs to be understood and transformed in me. Difficulties, both inner and outer, continue to be a fact of life, and opening to them rather than judging them as wrong always leads me to greater ease.

This attitude of acceptance is freeing when we apply it not only to our personal suffering but also to the suffering in the world. Once, as a young nun, when I was practicing a classic Plum Village guided meditation, I came to the final exercise, "Breathing in, I dwell in the present moment; breathing out, I know this is a wonderful moment." Suddenly I found myself stuck when I did this practice, questioning how we could truly affirm it was "a wonderful moment" with all the violence, hatred, inequality, and preventable tragedies that are happening in the present moment all over the world. It was a moment of truth, of genuinely feeling lost after I had been practicing this meditation for some years but now realizing I had not understood its deeper meaning.

I sat in the question of it and began to see that along with all the suffering and pain, there are also many beings that are supporting others in the present moment. There are many hearts of compassion, opening to relieve suffering, to care for others, to teach, to show a different way. There are people who are courageous and standing up for what they believe is right, protecting our oceans, cleaning rivers and beaches, advocating for those who are oppressed. There are those in every corner of the planet who are quietly doing the things no one else wants to do: caring for the forgotten people, places, species, and doing what needs to be done.

When I focused on that other part of the larger picture, I was able to touch that, yes, this present moment is also a wonderful moment. I saw that suffering doesn't have to disappear in order for beauty to be there. That life is about all of these things. It was a moment of cultivating acceptance and inclusiveness, opening myself to hold everything, all the paradoxes. The reality is that there is great terror and pain, and there is great love and great wisdom. They're all here, coexisting in this moment.

There is a teaching that says, "Pain is inevitable, but suffering is optional." Everyone has difficulty, no one can be immune to this, but how we respond to it, that's up to us. The Buddha taught that when pain comes to us, it's like we are hit with an arrow. But when we resist our pain, when we get stuck in blaming and judging, we are shooting ourselves with a second arrow in the same spot and it's much more painful than the first.

Ajahn Chah, the Thai Forest monk and teacher, asked his students one day when they passed a big boulder, "Do you think that boulder is heavy?" His students said, "Yes, it's extremely heavy." Then Ajahn Chah said, "Only if you try to pick it up!"

So, we can avoid unnecessarily picking up boulders when we let go of fighting the challenges in our lives. If we can change something, we should do it, without complaining, judging, or blaming. But if we can't do anything to change it, we can learn to accept it. Shantideva, the eighth-century Indian Buddhist monk and scholar, says it this way: "Why worry if you can do something about it? And why worry if you cannot do anything about it?"

Kittisaro, a teacher in the Vipassana tradition and a mentor of mine, shares this story in an interview from *The Sun* magazine about accepting what is, even when circumstances are difficult.

> Illness wasn't a teacher I would have chosen, but there was nothing I could do about it. Until that point, I had basically been able to accomplish whatever I wanted through willpower, study, and persistence. I'd been able to bend circumstances to my desires. My sense of self was intimately connected with my success.
>
> Then I spent years struggling with chronic pain, overpowering weakness, digestive disorders, internal bleeding, and so on. Though I saw doctors and healers and underwent myriad treatments, I couldn't overcome the illness. Unable to participate in the normal monastic routine, I felt like a failure. Fortunately, the Buddha taught that sickness, old age, and death are heavenly messengers, and that to live in denial of these truths results in suffering. My illness taught me how to die—in

other words, how to surrender to
what I couldn't change, and how to
make peace with the painful and
confused states of body and mind
that I encountered. My capacity for
patience deepened, and in moments
when I wasn't feeling sorry for myself
or wishing my life were otherwise,
I discovered that there is a deep part of
ourselves that is never sick, that never
dies. That unyielding illness, which
refused to follow my orders, brought
me to a place where I lost everything
I'd thought I was. Then I found what
remains, which no one can take away.[5]

We can soften when we are met with uncertainty. Acceptance is a profound practice of surrendering, letting go, leaning in toward. Not pushing against or stiffening. I invite you to consciously practice this now in your body. What might you be pushing away that you can soften toward and accept right in this moment?

MEDITATION

Accepting What Is

Let's begin our practice by finding a comfortable position of dignity and ease.

Let's really take our seats, let's really occupy this moment. If there are parts of ourselves somewhere else, in some other time, past or future, invite them all to come back. We'll be here, we'll be now. Settling into just being here. With all the tumult that may be in your life, still you can breathe in and out, with presence, recollecting yourself.

Feel the contact between your body and the floor, whether through the soles of your feet or your legs, knowing that the Earth is supporting you in this moment.

Allow the in-breath and the out-breath to flow naturally. Experience how the breath arrives, what happens as you breathe in. Feel how the out-breath just does what it does, quite naturally.

> *Breathing in, aware of the body. Breathing out,*
> *allowing the body to rest, calming the body.*
> *Aware of the body with the in-breath. Calming,*
> *resting, with the out-breath.*

. . .

If you notice that your mind wanders into thinking, planning, worrying, acknowledge that it is happening, knowing you can return to focus on your thoughts later. For now, engage again with the exercise of attending to this moment.

Inhale and open up to the awareness that this moment is enough, that what we need, it's already here. As you exhale, practice to accept that life is as it is in this moment. Allow it to be here, just as it is. Inhaling the sense of enoughness, of contentment, that actually things are okay right here and right now, we don't need anything more. Exhaling acceptance of how things are.

> *Breathing in enoughness, breathing out acceptance....*

. . .

If you feel very courageous today, maybe you'd like to try this exercise also, breathing with awareness with the following words:

> *Breathing in, I dwell in the present moment.*
> *Breathing out, I see that it is a wonderful moment.*
> *Present moment, wonderful moment.*

Take in the fullness of life, the many truths of this moment. Affirm the beauty and wonder of it in the midst of all the difficulty and suffering.

So, we practice to accept our situation as it is, whatever the awkwardness, discomfort, suffering, loss, or grief.

We can open ourselves to it, not resist it or push it away. That helps the pain already begin to lessen straightaway. Let your body physically soften the resistance, tension, blame, or judgment of this situation. We sit in acceptance, not shooting ourselves with a second arrow....

> Quiet friend who has come so far,
> feel how your breathing makes more
> space around you.
> Let this darkness be a bell tower
> and you the bell. As you ring,
> what batters you becomes your strength.
> Move back and forth into the change.
> What is it like, such intensity of pain?
> If the drink is bitter, turn yourself
> to wine.
>
> —Rainer Maria Rilke[6]

In Daily Life

You can bring this practice of acceptance into daily life by practicing to distinguish the first arrow, or the pain of an original difficult experience, from the second arrow, or the suffering that follows when we resist it. When challenges like disappointment, loneliness, illness, or loss arise, see if you can open to the original pain of that experience with acceptance, not pushing it away, so that you might avoid striking yourself with the second arrow of judgment, blame, and complaining.

You might explore setting the intention to consciously soften your body when you notice yourself stiffening in resistance to what is.

ooooo

In this third lesson we've explored the possibility of meeting challenges with acceptance, not avoiding or resisting pain but instead learning to open to it. We have practiced connecting to our experience and letting it be just as it is.

JOURNALING EXERCISE

How do you tend to respond to the first arrow of pain or difficulty when it hits you?

How would you like to respond?

What would support you in shifting your response?

Have you experienced accepting or opening to your difficulty?

What happened when you were able to do this?

Chapter 4

WEATHERING THE STORM

I must undertake to love myself and to respect myself
as though my very life depends upon self-love and
self-respect.

—June Jordan

Most of us walk without chains, yet we aren't free.
We're tethered to regret and sorrow from the past.
We return to the past and continue to suffer. The past is
a prison. But now you have the key to unlock the door
and arrive in the present moment. You breathe in, you
bring your mind home to your body, you make a step,
and you arrive in the here and the now.

—Thich Nhat Hanh,
How to Walk

I n my final years as a nun in the Plum Village community, I went through a time of real existential
crisis about what I should be doing with my life. I was
considering whether to leave the monastery, which, as
I have previously mentioned, was a huge question to be
holding. I had spent my whole adult life as a monastic

39

and had a clear identity and role as an elder sister in the community. Contemplating a future outside the monastery, I could see there was no clear path ahead of me, no job, no relationship, no community, no place to live, no security at all. And yet I couldn't stay in monastic robes just because it was comfortable and known. Something was calling to me that I couldn't ignore.

At the time, I was living at our center in Germany, where we were about to host two large retreats of about a thousand people each. Previously I had been quite involved in helping to run those annual retreats, but now I felt I couldn't manage to even be present during the retreats because of how confused I was feeling about my path. So, I asked my sisters if I could go to Plum Village, our monastery in France, during all the busyness of the retreats. They did not feel it was a good idea and requested me to ask Thay directly.

I went to Thay and said, "I have no space inside, and I cannot see myself staying here for these retreats. It's too much for me." He heard me out quietly, which he would always do, and then said, "Yes, I hear all that you are saying, *and* you can stay here." In other words, you're capable of staying.

I pressed on, insisting, "But it's so tight inside. I am totally up against a wall." He replied, "This is exactly the time when you take refuge in the basic practices of mindful sitting, breathing, and being aware of each step. Anytime you walk, you are aware you are taking this step; when you take a breath, you're aware you're taking this breath."

As I listened to him speak, I began to relax, and I realized he was right. He was seeing a capacity in me that I couldn't see in myself. I understood that I could in fact stay for the retreats. He made it clear that I didn't need to be on the frontlines, being in the public eye, facilitating a sharing group, or making announcements, and so on, but that I could just stay and be there with the community. I was willing to try.

After that, things became much more workable. Thay had given me a great gift with that teaching; his reminding me of the basic practices of mindful walking and mindful breathing helped me to weather that storm. And my experience of both retreats turned out to be affirming and empowering. I didn't have major responsibilities in the first retreat, but I was nourished by the energy of the community and participated in all the activities. By the second retreat I was ready to facilitate a group. I was in touch with how beautiful it is to be part of a large body of people practicing mindfulness and realized I had the capacity to persevere and find my center in the very midst of crisis and confusion. I wouldn't have learned that about myself if I had run away.

We can shift our experience of overwhelm by this basic practice of being with what is here and now. So much of the overwhelm and the stress comes from all that we are afraid might happen in the future. But in this moment, right here, there is the ability to recognize fear, to be with fear, and to not be swallowed by it. There is non-fear, and we can touch that. If we're running, then it's fear that's running the show. But if we can stop, we have the chance to touch into something deeper than the overwhelm.

So, I'd like to invite us to do together the basic practices Thay reminded me to return to in that stormy time in Germany. The first one we'll do is belly breathing.

Imagine a large tree in a storm. The top of the tree is waving about violently in the wind, but if you look down at the trunk of the tree, it's firm, very solid. It is the same with us. In times of emotional turmoil, it is dangerous to stay at the level of our mind, the upper branches. Feeding the thoughts of anxiety, anger, or despair can get us into real trouble. Instead, we can bring our attention down to our belly, the trunk of our tree, which is stable and steady. There we'll be safe. We bring all of our awareness to our belly and don't let our attention get caught up in the thrashing of the upper branches of our thinking mind. At least not until they calm down and the storm has passed.

MEDITATION

Belly Breathing

Let's try this out. Find a comfortable way to lie down on your back, either on the floor or on your bed. It can be helpful to place an object on your abdomen: a large book, a pound or half-kilogram bag of rice, a warm water bottle, or a cushion that weighs a few pounds. Only use the weight if it is comfortable. While easier to do lying down, you can also do this practice sitting or standing without the weight.

Begin to feel your breath, coming in and flowing out. Notice how your belly rises with the in-breath, and falls with the out-breath. Bring all of your attention to the rising and falling of your belly. Rising and falling.

If your mind gets pulled into the turmoil of thinking or strong emotions, bring it back, gently, kindly, to rest on the sensation of your belly rising and falling, rising and falling. Just that. The object resting on your belly can give you a stronger sensation of pressure so you can stay focused on the contact between the object and your belly, and follow the wave-like movements of the belly. As you breathe in, the wave comes in; as you breathe out, the wave rolls out. The wave rolls in, and the wave rolls out ... in, out. ... Stay here for some minutes or longer—as needed—until the storm has passed.

As you're ready, gently return to this moment.

· · ·

This is a very helpful practice to share with the young people in our lives—children, teens, or young adults. It can be a very useful tool in a time of crisis, and I have heard people share that it saved their life.

The next practice we will do is mindful walking or mindful moving.

When I first learned mindful walking, I was twenty-three years old, and I felt as if I'd never actually walked until then. I'd always been rushing to get to my destination, or walking while paying attention to my thoughts rather than to my body. I learned to make each step in awareness, and I became fully alive. I saw a little flower along the path and I knew it was smiling at me! I had to smile in return. I received the gift it had been trying to offer me for a long time, because finally I was truly there.

We can apply mindful moving to many challenging situations as well. I know of a family who was traveling with their small children to several countries on sabbatical. As you can imagine, long plane rides were difficult. When the youngest child was apt to start crying, the father practiced mindful walking, being aware of each step, with his toddler up and down the aisle of the airplane to help himself and his child calm down and weather the storm. Thay shares about how he practiced walking mindfully when he was in a serious depression after working to end the war in Vietnam and losing many beloved friends and students in the conflict. He said that practicing mindful walking for several hours a day helped him heal and come out of that depression.

MEDITATION

Walking or Moving Mindfully

So, how do we do it? You can do this practice walking or moving in a wheelchair or other assistive device. When we move in awareness, we begin moving a bit slower than usual, bringing all of our attention into our body. Either down to the soles of our feet, feeling the contact between our feet and the earth, or connecting with the contact between our body and our wheelchair or assistive device and its contact with the earth. We let ourselves rest in every movement or every step. We're not rushing into the future, but resting back in this moment, in this step, like we practiced in Chapter 2. All of our awareness is on just where we are right in this moment. Right here, right now.

Choose a place where you can move 5–7 yards back and forth, either indoors or outdoors. My friend Amana Brembry Johnson shares the following instructions she once heard from performance improvement specialist Matthew Huston:

> *As you move along, bring your awareness to the earth beneath the wheels. Is it smooth, or rough? Level, or slanted?*
> *Notice the differences in feeling when moving over*

*smooth concrete, or over bricks embedded in the
ground, or moving over grass, or the lines cut into
the concrete. Notice the transitions from rolling
over a rug onto a bare, hard surface or the crunch
of rocks against the tires.*

*How does the sound of the wheels change as the
surface changes? What are the effects of gravity
as you encounter an incline or decline? What
other aspects of the earth and of the experience of
moving along can you notice?*[7]

If you are walking, take your time to come to a standing position. Feel your feet on the ground as you stand.
Begin to take a few steps, slowly, with full awareness …
feel the way your body moves to allow a step to happen
… feel the shifting from one foot to the other … how
you are able to keep your balance … notice the movement of your body through space … let yourself relax
and enjoy your steps. … We are not trying to arrive
anywhere but right in the present moment.

If you like, you can also combine your breath with
your movements … notice how you breathe in as you
move a few inches or steps and then breathe out as you
move a few inches or steps … you could say "in" as you
breathe in and move forward or take a step, and "out"
as you breathe out and move forward or take a step …

Let your body release tension with every step, with
each moment …

Connect with the earth, feeling grounded …

You can kiss the Earth with every step, with every feeling of contact between your body, your wheelchair, and the earth … appreciating the Earth in all her wonder, that we even have an Earth to move on. Enjoy a gentle smile, imprinting your tenderness, peace, and freedom on the Earth with every movement or step … And if thoughts and worries arise, acknowledge them, and return your attention to the contact between you and the Earth. Or if your difficulties feel too big for you, you can move and invite the Earth to hold these difficulties with you. You are not alone; as you move, the Earth can support you and help you to release some of the burden by sharing it with you.

When you are ready, you can come to stillness. Continue to feel your body in the sitting or standing position. Breathing in, breathing out, be connected to the Earth, fully here in this place and time.

Wonderful. Good job!

> *Breathing in, I go back to the island within myself.*
> *There are beautiful trees within the island,*
> *there are clear streams of water, there are birds,*
> *sunshine, and fresh air.*
> *Breathing out, I feel safe.*
> *I enjoy going back to my island.*
>
> —Plum Village song
> "The Island Within"

In Daily Life

Mindful moving is a powerful practice to bring into everyday life. You may want to choose a short distance that you take each day, like from the door of your home to the street, or from your bedroom to the bathroom, and set the intention to remember to be aware of your movement or steps whenever you are taking that short path of 5-7 yards. Let those brief moments be a pause from the usual stream of thinking, planning, and worrying and just be a time of connecting with the wonder and physicality of each movement or step.

∞∞∞

In this fourth chapter, we have explored how we can develop faith in ourselves to endure and persevere when we think we have reached our limit. And we've learned how to weather the storms of our challenging times through the practice of belly breathing and mindful walking or moving.

JOURNALING EXERCISE

When you have encountered stormy times
in your life, what has helped you move
through them?

How did you experience the two meditations—
belly breathing and mindful walking/
moving—in this chapter?

In a time of overwhelm or difficulty, which
of the two meditations do you think you
could access most readily to help you weather
the storm?

Chapter 5

CARING FOR STRONG EMOTIONS

Without mud, there is no lotus. Without suffering, there's no happiness. So, we shouldn't discriminate against the mud. We have to learn how to embrace and cradle our own suffering and the suffering of the world, with a lot of tenderness.

—Thich Nhat Hanh,
No Mud, No Lotus: The Art of Transforming Suffering

The root of all fear is the fear of our painful emotions.

—Lama John Makransky

Buddhist psychology offers a model of the mind that divides our consciousness into two layers: the upper layer is "mind consciousness," our waking mind, and the lower layer is "store consciousness," similar to the concept of the unconscious in Western psychology. It is called "store consciousness" because it stores the potentialities of our mental states, which are described as seeds, sleeping in the depths of our mind. There are many kinds of seeds in our store consciousness, some wholesome, like mindfulness, generosity, and forgiveness, and some unwholesome, like greed, ignorance, and hatred. All of us have all of these many types of seeds.

Another way of thinking of these two layers is as a living room—the mind consciousness—and a basement—the store consciousness. When a seed is watered down in our store consciousness, or basement, it rises up into mind consciousness, or the living room, and manifests as an activated mental state, no longer sleeping, but capable of impacting our body and our actions, and changing our physiology. Suddenly we have a guest in the living room and depending on which guest it is, it can make our living room pleasant and cozy or very unpleasant and tense.

For example, if the seed of anger is watered, it wakes up from its sleeping state and becomes the mind state, or the energy, of anger. We feel heat and constriction, and maybe more blood begins flowing to our extremities, preparing us to fight, flee, or freeze. In this state, if we are not aware, we think, say, and do things that express our irritation and anger, often to our chagrin later.

Every minute we spend consuming or expressing anger makes the seed of anger in the basement grow slightly bigger. The next time something happens to trigger our anger, it arises faster from the basement, is more intense, and stays longer in the living room. If we keep allowing the seed of anger to be watered (either by ourselves or by our environment), we get stuck in a toxic loop that makes it grow bigger and bigger every day and we become trapped in a pattern of constantly getting angered by even small things that didn't bother us before. This is detrimental to our body and mind; our nervous system was not designed to handle such stress.

However, we also have the seed of mindfulness in our store consciousness, down in the basement. We can call up this seed whenever we want. It is always there, always available. One mindful breath, in and out, one step made in full awareness, is enough to bring up the seed of mindfulness and it becomes present in our living room as the energy of mindfulness. It has a soothing, refreshing effect on our body and mind, bringing attentiveness, friendliness, and curiosity to our experience.

Often, we either suppress our painful emotions like anger or shame by avoiding them, pretending they aren't there, or we vent them, letting them run the show and take over our living room. Neither of these approaches helps us to transform these emotions or mind states at their root in store consciousness.

Mindfulness is a middle way, a third option that actually leads us to transformation and peace. We can care for any of our strong emotions like anger, jealousy, sadness, confusion, or fear, by calling mindfulness up into the living room as soon as we notice that an unwholesome seed has arisen. We say to ourselves, "Breathing in, I know I am angry; breathing out, I am here for my anger." We don't deny our anger or try to distract ourselves from it with technology or consuming something. We turn towards it, we face it. It can help to be aware of how it feels in the body, noticing where we feel it and what its physical characteristics are.

When we do this, immediately our painful emotion begins to settle down somewhat, because we're not pushing it away. There's no war within us. We're being honest with ourselves, and returning home to take care of the tense situation in the living room.

I had this experience once when I woke up at 4:00 a.m. I lay in bed thinking of all the things that I needed to resolve in my life. My body began to tense up unconsciously. Because of all my thinking, I worried I wouldn't be able to fall back asleep. After about twenty minutes of this, I suddenly recognized what was happening. I realized, "Ah! This is worry!" Then mindfulness was there in the living room, not just worry. As soon as I could identify the emotion, I began to feel much better. "I see you, worry," I said to myself. I was no longer unconsciously bracing against it, and fighting it or fearing it unawares. I brought awareness to my body and my breathing, and released the tension bit by bit. I gave it space and was able to return to a state of deep rest.

Once mindfulness recognizes anger, it begins to accept it and give it space. We open to our experience of anger and allow it to be here. We generate compassion for ourselves, recognizing anger is a part of us so we don't want to reject or judge it. However, accepting anger doesn't mean we give it freedom to cause destruction. Mindfulness is there with it in the living room, so it can do no harm.

When we've accepted it, we embrace it, like an older sibling or caretaker might hold a crying baby. We acknowledge that this part of us is suffering and we move closer, opening our arms to take good care of it. We hold it, rock it, soothe it. We can even speak to this part of ourselves as we practice, saying, "My dear anger, I'm here for you, holding you with my mindfulness. I will stay here and take good care of you, not leaving you alone or denying you. You are a part of me and I'm here to embrace you with my kindness and concern."

As we do this, our anger calms down. After a while, it will begin to reveal itself to us, and we will see below the surface, into its depths. We will begin to understand where it comes from; for instance, it may not even be our own anger, but may be the anger of our ancestors, or of our community, our nation. And when we understand it better, we are better able to help it release. In this step we investigate the experience of anger, and it leads us to insight into our deeply held patterns and the transformation of our behavior and attitudes.

When we practice caring for the energy of anger with mindfulness in this way, the seed of anger gets smaller at the root and the next time something upsets us, anger is slower to arise, it is less intense, and it passes more quickly. In this way, anger, or any strong emotion, begins to have an ever-weaker hold on us, and we become more and more free. As Dan Emmons says, "What most needs attention is the part of us that we seek to avoid feeling. When we have tended to that, we are changed, and the world changes with us."

MEDITATION

Caring for Strong Emotions

In this meditation on embracing strong emotions, I will invite you to bring to mind a slightly difficult or challenging moment that you experienced recently, but not a major or particularly traumatic one. It is best to begin with what is easier. Or you could bring to mind a situation that happened some time ago but that involves a sticky or difficult emotion you often encounter in your life and are curious about.

Note: If at any point you feel overwhelmed, pause the meditation, open your eyes, connect with the places your body is making contact with, or bring awareness to the colors and shapes in your environment. You can change your bodily position and stretch. If after this, you feel more settled you can resume the practice or shift instead to mindfulness of the body or breath.

Find a comfortable position, letting the body open and settle. Feel the solidity and stability of the Earth and let it hold you. Allow your body to rest within the support of the Earth.

Connect with the experience of breathing in and out.

Enjoy the natural flow of the breath, how it knows just what to do. There's no need to manage it, it takes care of itself.

Let your attention sweep through your body now to release places of holding or tension, your face, jaw, shoulders, belly ... any other places that might need your attention. Notice if there are places in the body that feel good, pleasant, or neutral, where things are just okay.

It can be helpful to first resource yourself, so bring to mind a place, person, or animal that helps you feel safe and connected. Visualize the characteristics of this being or place. Connect with the positive feelings you have when you are close to this being or in this place. Breathe these feelings into your body and mind and allow them to nourish you.

Now allow the difficult emotion to be here. Imagine yourself back in that situation and notice what emotion or emotions arose. Was it anger, worry, fear, sadness, doubt, shame, disappointment, something else? Whatever it was, notice how it feels in you now. What are its qualities? Is it heavy, sticky, sharp, dull, aching, hot, or cold?

Allow mindfulness to also come up now and be with your emotion. With mindfulness you breathe in and out, recognizing the emotion, calling it by name, becoming familiar with it. Stay present with it.

Breathe in and out, staying focused on what you experience in your body. Mindful awareness offers acceptance to this painful emotion. While part of you may want to run away from the pain, mindfulness is here and is helping you to give it space, to offer it friendship. Feel yourself opening to accept and befriend this painful emotion to whatever extent you can.

Now, with this gentle opening toward your experience, you can embrace this part of you, accepting it even more deeply. Open your arms to it and offer love and care, like you would hold a crying baby who just needs compassion and care. Release any judgment toward your emotion and see if you can bring in the energy of tenderness. "My dear emotion, I am here for you, holding you. I will take good care of you. I won't leave you or abandon you." Let yourself express whatever wants to come to this part of yourself that has been rejected so many times. Now it is finally getting the care it needs.

Take several deep breaths as you bring an attitude of embracing to this part of yourself and notice how this feels in your body.

Now turn with interest to explore what this emotion has come to teach you. What wisdom does it hold? What has brought it about? Maybe some part of it reveals itself to you that you hadn't seen or understood before. Look deeply into it to see it more clearly. What might this emotion need or want from you right now?

Wonderful. Really good. Now let yourself settle back and rest, opening to whatever is here in your body, in your awareness after doing this exercise. Allow the insight or transformation you experienced some space and time to integrate.

> *Hello weeds, hello garbage, hello future compost.*
> *Thank you for this chance for transformation, I'm*
> *so happy that you're here.*
> *If I hide you away, you'll just come back bigger*
> *anyway,*
> *So, I'll take care of you, and soon you'll be beautiful*
> *flowers.*

—"Hello Weeds" song

We don't need to get rid of the 'weeds' in us; in fact, they are essential, they become fertile compost for the garden of our mind. With mindfulness, anger can turn into compassion, greed into generosity, and ignorance into wisdom. These difficult emotions in us are like mud that is helping the lotus of awakening to grow. They have a fundamental place and as we learn to work skillfully with them, they transform into exquisite flowers.

In Daily Life

Whenever a strong emotion arises in daily life, see if you can remember the first step, to recognize it. Bring mindfulness up from store consciousness to accompany the strong emotion. Feel where it is in your body. Notice what sensations it has. Practice saying hello to your strong emotion and calling it by name, saying, "I see you, worry/sadness/irritation, I know you are here," as soon as possible once you are aware it has arisen in your mind. If you can't identify it, that's okay. You can just say, "Suffering or discomfort is here." This way you have a choice about how to respond to the strong emotion, rather than being taken over by it.

∞∞∞∞

In this fifth chapter, we learned about and practiced the five steps of caring for strong emotions:

Recognize the strong emotion.

Accept it.

Embrace it.

Look deeply into it.

Allow insight to arise.

JOURNALING EXERCISE

What general category of strong emotions do you find yourself faced with most in this time of transition and challenge?

Frustration, anger
Sadness, despair
Confusion, ambivalence
Anxiety, fear
Something else

What is your habitual response
to this strong emotion?

How was it for you to approach this difficult emotion with kindness and friendliness?

Chapter 6

IMPERMANENCE
AND THE FIVE
REMEMBRANCES

It is the responsibility of free [people] to trust and to celebrate what is constant—birth, struggle, and death are constant, and so is love, though we may not always think so—and to apprehend the nature of change, to be able and willing to change. I speak of change not on the surface but in the depths—change in the sense of renewal. But renewal becomes impossible if one supposes things to be constant that are not— safety, for example, or money or power. One clings then to chimeras, by which one can only be betrayed, and the entire hope—the entire possibility—of freedom disappears.

—James Baldwin,
The Fire Next Time

O ur whole lives are a process of transition. Even in relatively stable times when we may spend a few years or more in the same dwelling, relationship, job, or place of study, we are still constantly changing—from one breath to another, morning to night, from week to week, month to month. About one hundred million new red blood cells are being formed in our bodies every minute! Our bodies and minds are changing in every moment, just in subtler ways than the bigger transitions we go through.

Impermanence is one of the key marks of existence. It influences everything. Recognizing how it constantly operates in our lives in small, everyday ways helps us to be more receptive and accepting of how it operates in larger ways, in times of bigger upheaval and turmoil: times of loss, changes in our relationships, work, living environment, or health.

Many of us may get lulled into believing what we have now will always be here. This is a central cause of our suffering. We want that which has the nature to change to stay the same. For those of us living in Western cultures that are obsessed with youth and that avoid or try to hide the reality of death from us, this very human tendency is only further underscored.

But facing the truth of impermanence actually frees us up to live our lives more deeply and to transform our deepest fears. Our fear of change and resistance to change are sleeping just beneath the surface; the more we can bring them into conscious awareness and make a point to look at them clearly, the less we will be controlled by them operating under the radar of awareness.

Impermanence is not an idea but an insight. An insight that can be enormously empowering because we're opening to the truth of how life is, not remaining confused by our delusions and how we want it to be. We can observe it in the constant changing of our breath, the flow of the in- and the out-breath, how no breath is the same as a breath that came before, just like no moment is the same as one that came before. We can see it in the unfolding of our life span and the life spans of those we love. Spending time in nature, we notice the constant changing in animals, plants, weather, the cyclical movement of time. And we can also observe it on a larger scale in the evolution of our human species, all species, the profound changes that planet Earth has gone through, not to mention the changes in solar systems, galaxies, and the entire universe. Everything is constantly in flux.

The Buddha offered a meditation on impermanence to help shake us out of our dream that things will stay the same, as we wish them to. Called the Five Remembrances, this contemplation asks us to remember five things every day: that we are of the nature to grow old, to have ill health, and to die, that our loved ones are of the nature to change and we can't avoid being separated from them, and lastly, that our actions are our only true possessions, we don't get to take anything else with us when we pass away.[8]

In this meditation practice, we consciously bring up the things that we usually don't want to see: that we and those we love will one day pass away. Thay says contemplating impermanence in this way is not intended to make us feel depressed or anxious but to actually help us feel more alive and in touch with life. To appreciate its preciousness even more.

I offered these Five Remembrances to teenagers on a teen retreat some years ago and they reflected that this meditation was painful but good. They experienced it as refreshing, opening them up so that they could live deeply and treasure their relationships more fully.

Mindfulness practice is also a preparation for one of the biggest transitions and challenges we will each face: our own death. When we meditate on the Five Remembrances, we are preparing ourselves so that we will know one day how to die well. Meditating on them can also help us to be ready to support and accompany others when they pass away. This is a very precious gift, to help someone experience some measure of acceptance or non-fear in the face of death.

Another major transition is the huge one our species is now facing with the climate crisis. While this may be quite overwhelming to contemplate, purposely turning toward impermanence and accepting this as our reality can help us to make decisions that will help us face the possibility of societal collapse with more resilience and adaptability. As James Baldwin says, "Not everything that is faced can be changed, but nothing can be changed until it is faced." While these five practices are framed individually, we can also apply them to our collective: just as our societies, cultures, governments are of the nature to come into being, evolve, and change, they are also of the nature to grow old, sicken, and fall away. We need to face this truth of impermanence at the collective level.

So, let's begin this practice of facing the truth about our lives. If you notice discomfort or fear arising as you do the meditation, pause to be with and care for these difficult emotions with compassion and kindness. You can pause at any time to be present for whatever needs your attention.

MEDITATION

The Five Remembrances

Settle into a position that's supportive and comfortable. Feel your breath. Feel your body. Let yourself begin to open and settle as you drop into this moment. Give yourself a few minutes in silence to breathe with and contemplate each of the exercises that follow.

> *I am of the nature to grow old.*
> *There is no way to escape growing old.*

Visualize yourself aging, becoming an elderly person, or even more elderly than you are, if you're already an elder. See your body, see your face, let yourself really contemplate the process of growing older. Old age will happen to you. Notice any response to this in your body and bring kindness and care to what you sense.

You can breathe in and recollect: "Growing old," and breathe out and recollect: "No escape."

Breathing in, growing old,
Breathing out, no escape.

Practice with this in silence for a few minutes.

I am of the nature to have ill health.
There is no way to escape having ill health.

Now contemplate yourself in some situation in which you're dealing with illness, whether physical or psychological, when people may need to help you and take care of you. Or you're unable to do the things you're normally able to do. Let that in, that that's part of life. There's no escape from ill health. Notice any response to this in your body and bring kindness and curiosity to what you are feeling.

Breathing in, ill health,
Breathing out, no escape.

. . .

I am of the nature to die.
There is no way to escape death.

Picture yourself on your deathbed, the last moments of your life. Taking your final breaths. Feel into how you want those moments to be. Peaceful, calm, free from fear? Know that every time you bring up the awareness of your own death now, while you're fully alive, you nourish the seed in you of being able to face your death with strength, with clarity, with tranquility. Really let yourself take in that one day you will die, one day you will take your very last breath. There's no escape from death. Notice whatever sensations may be there in response to this in your body and bring gentleness and curiosity to what you are feeling.

> *Breathing in, dying,*
> *Breathing out, no escape*

. . .

> *All that is dear to me and everyone I love are of*
> *the nature to change.*
> *There is no way to escape being separated*
> *from them.*

Again, visualize yourself having to be separated from what you love, people, places, things, and how they will all change. There's no way to escape being separated from them. Allow that in, accept that truth. Again, notice whatever sensations may be there in response to this in your body and bring kindness and curiosity to what you are feeling.

Breathing in, all that is dear to me will change,
Breathing out, no escape from being separated
from those I love

. . .

My actions are my only true belongings.
I cannot escape the consequences of my actions.
My actions are the ground on which I stand.

Bring awareness to the fact that when we pass away, we can't take anything with us. All we have are the consequences of our actions, and there's no escape from these consequences. Contemplate how you wish to live today with this in mind.

Breathing in, my actions are the only thing I take
with me,
Breathing out, there's no escape from the
consequences of my actions

. . .

Now let yourself rest back, connecting with your breathing, connecting with your body as you dwell in this moment.

. . .

There ain't no way to avoid dyin' for I am of the
nature to grow old,
There ain't no way to avoid sickness for I'm of the
nature to take ill.
All those dear and precious to me will change and
grow in their own time.
My actions are my true possessions, they are the
ground on which I stand.

— "Five Remembrances" song

In Daily Life

You can practice remembering impermanence throughout the day. You might pay particular attention to the
moments when you finish things. Whether it is a bev-
erage, a meal, a conversation, sending an email, or some
other activity, try pausing briefly to notice it has ended,
recognizing its impermanence. When you wake up, you
can bring to mind the Five Remembrances to help you
keep them in your awareness throughout the day. Quietly reflect: what actions do you want to take (or not
take) today knowing they are your only true possessions,
the ground on which you stand?

ooooo

In this sixth chapter we have explored the intrinsi-
cally impermanent nature of reality and how practices
of purposely contemplating impermanence can help us
live more deeply and release our fear.

JOURNALING EXERCISE

Does one of the Five Remembrances resonate
with you more than others? Is there one that you
feel more uncomfortable with?

What comes up for you when you contemplate
impermanence and the Five Remembrances?
Do any of the responses below resonate
with you?

*I feel discomfort and shock, even though
logically I know they are true*

*I really don't want to go there; I numb out
or find this depressing*

*I can open to this reality somewhat
though it is still uncharted territory*

*I am comfortable reflecting on impermanence
and find it liberating*

Write about why you answered the way you did.

Chapter 7

CALMLY FACING THE EIGHT WORLDLY WINDS

My sisters.
The thing that breaks
and leaves sharp edges
that cut you from the inside—
that's not the heart.
That's the house you built
out of all the pretty things
other people told you,
and the strange promise
that what is felt today
will still be felt tomorrow.
But such houses are built to fall apart.
And when they do,
the heart must take to the open road
and leave the past behind.

...

Look me in the eye, my sister.
You are more than your laughter
and your sighs.
You are more than your rage
and your tears.
You are much more than your body.

        —Matty Weingast, "Chapa—The
        Archer" from *The First Free Women:
        Inspired by the Early Buddhist Nuns*[9]

I n many countries across Asia, in Buddhist temples you find a common symbol of a wheel with eight spokes, with a hole in the center for the axle. I learned that this represents the Dharma, or the teachings of the Buddha, which are like a wheel being set in motion, and the eight spokes represent the Noble Eightfold Path taught by the Buddha.

While living in Sri Lanka, I was offered an additional meaning of this symbol: the eight spokes represent the eight worldly winds. They are four pairs of opposites—pleasure and pain, gain and loss, praise and blame, and fame and disrepute. They are the four things we hope for and the four things we fear. The wheel of these eight winds is always turning. It never stops. So, we can't get comfortable with the joys of pleasure and gain, nor should we identify with the misfortunes that come our way and think they define our whole life. If we get possessive of them, we will get rope burn when they inevitably move on, and we will suffer if we think we can control them. The wheel is going to keep turning no matter what we do or how we live our lives. This doesn't mean our choices don't matter, or that ethical living is not important, but that even as we align ourselves with compassion and non-harming, we release the expectation that virtuous actions will always be rewarded or that the eight worldly winds will stop blowing and changing.

This teaching can help us face the ever-changing reality of our lives more gracefully because these winds do not blow in response to our actions, they are not necessarily deserved, whether pleasant or painful. Oppression, for instance, is never justified and it is not destined. When those with power oppress others, this injustice should be resisted and transformed. The changing nature of life's circumstances is not an excuse to avoid actively responding to and disrupting social injustice, to sidestep our responsibility to speak up.

When we can do something to change things, we must. But sometimes there is nothing we can do to shift the situation. In both cases, it brings spaciousness to remember that "life is full of ups and downs," as the beloved Cambodian monk Mahagosananda said in response to being asked how he maintained his balance and optimism during the terror of the Khmer Rouge. When we accept that this is life, we are able to touch that we are more than our life's ups and downs.

Thay has offered us Six Mantras of True Love:

> *My darling, I am here for you.*
> *My darling, I know you are there, and I am*
> *very happy.*
> *My darling, I know you suffer, that is why*
> *I'm here for you.*
> *My darling, I suffer, and I need your help.*
> *My darling, this is a happy moment.*
> *My darling, you are partly right.*

You can read more about them in Thich Nhat Hanh's book *Teachings on Love.*[10] We are to practice the sixth mantra, "You are partly right," whenever someone praises us or blames us. It has the wisdom of the eight worldly winds in it because we take neither the praise nor the blame as the complete description of who we are. When people appreciate us and affirm us, we know they see some part of us, our strengths, but we also know we have many weaknesses, so they are partly right. Similarly, when others judge and blame us, they may see our shortcomings clearly, but we also know we have our beauty and goodness, so they are just partly right. Practicing this mantra keeps us humble when we might fall into pride and also grounds us in confidence when we might fall into self-criticism. It helps us remember that the wheel is ever turning.

It's the hole in the center of the wheel that holds the key. It is empty. From the center we can see all the eight worldly winds without being caught up in them. And that center is a reminder of our own emptiness, which gives us the ability to see ourselves as more than these eight worldly winds that come our way. To, in fact, see ourselves in everyone and everything and see everyone and everything in us.

Thomas Merton speaks to this emptiness from the perspective of the contemplative Christian tradition:

> At the center of our being is a point
> of nothingness which is untouched
> by sin and by illusion, a point of pure
> truth, a point or spark which belongs

entirely to God, which is never at our
disposal, from which God disposes
of our lives, which is inaccessible to
the fantasies of our own mind or the
brutalities of our own will. This little
point of nothingness and of absolute
poverty is the pure glory of God in
us.... It is like a pure diamond, blazing
with the invisible light of heaven. It
is in everybody, and if we could see it,
we would see these billions of points
of light coming together in the face
and blaze of a sun that would make all
the darkness and cruelty of life vanish
completely.... I have no program for
this seeing. It is only given. But the gate
of heaven is everywhere.[11]

So, the gate of heaven is not in praise or gain if it is
not also in blame and loss. If we over-identify with the
eight winds and are dependent on other people's praise
or opinions about us to be happy, our happiness will be
insecure and unreliable. But if we can see our lives from
the standpoint of that empty center, that "point of pure
truth," we naturally then have compassion for ourselves
and the situations we encounter. And when the way
we see ourselves is based on our own compassion and
love for ourselves, which allows us to be forgiving of
our mistakes and confident in our progress on our path,

our happiness is solid and reliable. This non-reliance on external sources of approval and disapproval that float on the eight worldly winds brings us into our center, to the place of stillness and quiet that leads us to awareness of not-self.

We spoke in the last chapter about impermanence, a fundamental characteristic of existence. In Buddhism, not-self is another characteristic. That is the emptiness that the hole in the wheel represents.

Not-self means we are empty of a separate self, but full of everything else. We are made up of all those who have influenced us and helped shape us in some way: our parents, teachers, friends, the food we've eaten, the books we've read, sunlight, water, air. We cannot exist by ourselves alone. We can only exist because each of these elements has come to help make up part of who we are. If we can understand and live from this insight, we will be incredibly empowered and will hold a kind of secret weapon when moving through times of adversity and change. With the insight of not-self, we neither chase after pleasure or fame, nor fear pain or disrepute, because we know we are larger than these forces and they can't define us. This non-fear is what gives people courage to make big sacrifices and take incredible risks, knowing we are acting on behalf of the whole, and that our actions will still have an impact even if we, in our small selves, will not be there to see it. Brazilian theologian Rubem Alves says, "We must live by the love of what we will never see."

Another helpful analogy is that of waves and water. On one level a wave can be characterized as fast or slow, big or small, high or low. But if a wave is able to touch its true nature of water, it gets in touch with a part of itself that cannot be characterized by up or down, coming or going, being born or dying. Water is beyond all of these conditions. And so the empty hole of the wheel points us back to our true nature, not as a wave whipped about by the eight worldly winds, but rather as the water itself, vast and imperturbable.

When we touch our deeper reality as water, the insight of not-self, we navigate transitions much more easily. We do not take things as personally and we're less afraid. At the age of eighty-eight Thay had a massive stroke. The physicians didn't expect him to pull through. But he did. One side of his body was paralyzed, and he lost the ability to speak. He became totally dependent on others to take care of all of his needs. At first it must have been very difficult to adjust but now he seems to be at peace with his situation. I had a chance to visit him in Vietnam. In 2019, five years after his stroke, I experienced him as deeply present and spiritually powerful. I sense that he was able to move gracefully with the worldly winds of loss and pain because he wasn't attached to an idea of a separate self who had to try to maintain control and "keep it all together."

When we touch our nature as water, as the hole in the wheel, we get a larger perspective. We are not just these small selves in these limited circumstances. We are much, much more. As Thay wrote, "To see one in all and all in one is to break through the great barrier which narrows one's perception of reality."

MEDITATION

Facing the Eight Worldly Winds

Let's settle back into this moment, finding a supportive posture.

You can visualize your upper body, from your waist up, reaching toward the sky, like a tree. Now allow the lower part of your body to root down into the earth. Feel the aliveness in your body in this moment as you ground into the earth and grow upwards to the sky.

Allowing your whole body, your whole being to simply be and rest.

· · ·

Now let yourself sit in the center of the wheel, in that empty space where you can observe all the eight worldly winds blowing in and out. Though the wheel turns and turns, the eye of the wheel is still, and that's where you are. You observe the circumstances of your life, the losses, the gains, the pleasure, the pain, but you are beginning to get free from attachment and aversion to these things. Breathe deeply and let yourself rest in the still center, jumping off the endless and exhausting hamster wheel for a time. Open up and rest here.

· · ·

And now see yourself as a wave on the ocean. You rise up out of the water and begin to move quickly. And there are also other waves around you. The other waves around you are moving more slowly. You feel special because you can go faster. But then a huge wave comes by, dwarfing you and passing you by, making you feel small and insignificant.

But you and the slower waves, and you and the faster, bigger waves are actually of the same nature. Let go of your wave form and go beneath the surface and sink down, down, down. Now you are ready to rest into the embrace of the ocean and you touch the truth of your nature as water. Here, there is no fast or slow, big or small, there is just water, the same substance that makes up the waves that were slower than you and the wave that was bigger than you. Wait a second, there is no more you because now you're just water. Let yourself enjoy being immense, vast, empty of a separate self, content to contain everything around you.

> *I cannot add more days to my life, but only more life to each day.*
>
> —Plum Village song

In Daily Life

Whenever you face praise or blame, you may like to try practicing the sixth mantra: "You are partly right." Let yourself hear the praise or blame you receive and truly take them in, being willing to learn from them when they contain important feedback, and being nourished by them when they affirm you. But also see yourself in the center of the wheel, or at the depths of the ocean, knowing you are more than this assessment of you.

ooooo

In this seventh chapter we have learned how to keep ourselves from being blown about by the eight worldly winds. We have learned how cultivating the insight of not-self frees us right in the midst of the vicissitudes of life.

JOURNALING EXERCISE

Which of these pairs of the eight worldly winds is most relevant to what you are going through at this moment, or which has been a significant issue for you in your life?

Pleasure and pain
Gain and loss
Praise and blame
Fame and disrepute

In the midst of these ups and downs, how might you dwell in the space at the center of the wheel?

What support might you need for this and how might you get it?

Chapter 8

EQUANIMITY AND LETTING GO

Full of trust you left home,
and soon learned to walk the Path—
making yourself a friend to everyone
and making everyone a friend.
When the whole world is your friend,
fear will find no place to call home.
And when you make the mind your friend,
you'll know what trust
really means.
Listen.
I have followed this Path of friendship to its end.
And I can say with absolute certainty—
it will lead you home.

— Matty Weingast, "Mitta—
Friend" from *The First Free
Women: Poems of the Early
Buddhist Nuns*

W hen I was a child, I had a toy called a Weeble. It
was shaped like an egg and made of plastic. There
was some kind of weight in the bottom that kept it balanced and centered. You could tip it over and it seemed

like it would fall, but then it wouldn't. It rocked back and forth, and always came back upright to stillness.

What is it that allows us to come back to balance when the transitions and challenges of our life knock us off center? What is that inner weight at our core?

Equanimity is a fundamental practice that can help us to center and balance ourselves. The word in Sanskrit is *upeksha* (upekṣā), and in Pali it's *upekkha*. *Upe* means "over" and *ksa* means "to look." So upeksha means to look over, to see all around, like from a high mountain, to see all sides. From this standpoint we don't take sides, as we see the situation in its entirety. It can also mean to see with patience, to see with understanding and spacious-ness. It is sometimes translated as nondiscrimination, impartiality, tolerance, letting go, and nonattachment (which is distinct from indifference). Thay translates upeksha as *inclusiveness*, which gives a more engaged, involved, and active nuance to this quality.

Inclusiveness or equanimity is not dogmatic; it allows us to keep an open mind. When climbing a ladder, to advance to the next rung, we must let go of the rung we're standing on. We need to let go of what we know now to be open to learning something new. The willingness to see things afresh, with new eyes, is an important aspect of equanimity and inclusiveness. The Dalai Lama says, "I'll give up any Buddhist belief if science proves it wrong." As central as the practice and teachings of Buddhism have been for him and his culture, he won't cling to them. Because clinging prevents us from growing and moving forward.

Thay invites us to ask ourselves often, "Are you sure?" It is good to regularly check if our perceptions actually correspond with reality, because often they don't. We are usually looking only from one side of the mountain, not seeing from the top, so we are unable to see the whole situation with impartiality.

When we find ourselves in times of transition or difficulty, what are some ways we may be clinging to the current rung of our ladder? What might it be like to relax our grip and be willing to move to the next rung? Inclusiveness, equanimity helps us trust that we will be okay, even if right now it's uncomfortable or even hardly bearable. The more we can relax and let go the easier it will be.

Some years ago, my mom and I visited a museum to see an interactive exhibit on the brain. We played a game in which we had to sit across a table from each other and compete to try to get our particular ball to go the furthest distance. To do this, we had to relax. We were wearing sensors on a headband that measured our level of relaxation. So, the more relaxed we were, the quicker our ball would move where we wanted it to go. It was very counterintuitive! We laughed a lot. Often life is like that; the more we relax, settle back, and move with the flow of things, the more we advance where we want to go.

In order to relax, we need to let go and stop clinging. In the game, the ball doesn't advance because we are trying hard, it advances because we let go. Ajahn Chah, the Thai Forest monk, said, "If you let go a little, you will have a little freedom; if you let go a lot, you will have a lot of freedom; and if you let go completely, you will have complete freedom."

But this letting go doesn't mean indifference or not caring. It doesn't mean you don't love all your children—it means you love all of your children without discrimination. It also means we don't discriminate between ourselves and others. If I see myself as the one who loves and the other as the one who is loved, if I somehow see myself as superior or separate from the other, that's not true equanimity.

We can see equanimity as similar to grandmotherly love, which is more peaceful than the love of a parent because it's not as attached. The love is there, but without as much of the suffering. Equanimity helps us to take a longer, bigger view. Each person has their own journey, their own path to walk; we don't always see the logic of their trajectory. We can't see what it is that they need to go through in their life to learn the lessons they need to learn, to grow in the ways they need to grow. With the spaciousness of equanimity, we are able to see that this life is made up of what in Daoism is called "the ten thousand joys and the ten thousand sorrows." All the beauty, the happiness, the wonder, the connection, the belonging, and all the separation, the anxiety, the depression, the despair—that is a human life. It doesn't mean we don't try to alleviate suffering when it can be alleviated. But we touch great freedom when we can accept suffering as part of the path and not a mistake. With equanimity, we can know how not to make things worse when pain comes; we can choose not to add to the pain by resisting, suppressing, or judging it. Instead, we can choose to open to it, to allow for the fact that a certain measure of pain is part of life.

Equanimity keeps us grounded and cool so that we don't burn out in our caring, in our work to relieve suffering. Without equanimity, we can outpour to an extent that we become exhausted or overly identified with the situation. Equanimity can help keep us resourced and in our center. We need this coolness of equanimity because there's so much heat in the world right now—and it's only getting hotter. In light of the attempted coup on January 6, 2021, and other instances of political violence in the US, how do we relate to these forces with clarity and fierce compassion, calling those involved to justice without dehumanizing them? How do we see from all sides and include them in our hearts? Equanimity can help us not discriminate, and let go of the tendency to see ourselves as separate from others.

My dad has had quite a long journey with social justice work. He is a Christian minister who worked with Dr. King and the Southern Christian Leadership Conference on desegregating the South, then spent thirty years working in human and village development around the world, living several years in India, the Philippines, and Kenya. He went on to teach psychosynthesis-based unconditional love and forgiveness in workshops and retreats, and also became a devoted student of Thich Nhat Hanh. He was ordained as a Buddhist Dharma teacher in 2008. Over twenty-four years ago, he started a Sangha, a meditation group, that still continues to meet weekly. In a recent conversation, he and I were reflecting on the need to keep our balance. He said, "When we see ourselves as victims, that is the separate self. When we see ourselves as beloved, that is no-self." When we see ourselves as beloved, full of loving kindness, we see ourselves in everyone and everyone in ourselves; and we have a force with which to meet the ignorance, discrimination, and even violence in others so that it doesn't cripple us by making us hateful. When we see ourselves as beloved, we are in opposition to no one.

During the war in Vietnam, Thich Nhat Hanh said that other people are not our enemies, that a human is never our enemy. Our only enemies are delusion, hatred, and ignorance. It is possible to uproot this in ourselves and others. If we see ourselves as beloved, not as victims, we can encounter others without malice, even when we disagree. That's the power of equanimity, of inclusiveness.

Dr. Martin Luther King, Jr. offered this exhortation in his essay "Loving Your Enemies":

> To our most bitter opponents we say:
> "We shall match your capacity to inflict
> suffering by our capacity to endure
> suffering. We shall meet your physical
> force with soul force. Do to us what

you will, and we shall continue to love you. We cannot in all good conscience obey your unjust laws, because noncooperation with evil is as much a moral obligation as is cooperation with good. Throw us in jail, and we shall still love you. Bomb our homes and threaten our children, and we shall still love you. Send your hooded perpetrators of violence into our community at the midnight hour and beat us and leave us half dead, and we shall still love you. But be ye assured that we will wear you down by our capacity to suffer. One day we shall win freedom, but not only for ourselves. We shall so appeal to your heart and conscience that we shall win you in the process, and our victory will be a double victory.[12]

This, too, is the voice of equanimity. A voice much needed in our deeply divided world. This practice of equanimity, of inclusiveness, can give us great courage. The Buddha said that when you have equanimity, you have a mind of immeasurable peace. When you have peace, you have a lot of freedom. And when you have freedom, you're not so afraid.

After hearing the verdict in the Derek Chauvin trial, I was extremely relieved. The horrific suffering of

George Floyd, calling out for his mother as his life was being extinguished, was gut-wrenching and enraging to witness. And I knew, like many others, that the wound of George Floyd's murder could not be healed by this guilty ruling alone. I meditated on the insight of inclusiveness and what it would mean to touch not only the agony and injustice endured by George Floyd and his family and the families of all those Black and brown people killed by police, but also to touch the reality inhabited by Derek Chauvin and the far-too-numerous police officers involved in racialized terror and the killings of innocent people. Pondering Derek Chauvin's mugshot, I thought he looked profoundly lost.

Whenever we dehumanize another, we are cut off from our own humanity as well. I reflected on the fact that Derek Chauvin was a few years younger than George Floyd. I wondered what they both might have been like as young boys, how they might have played together. I thought about the consequences Derek Chauvin now has to live with, and wondered if he would ever understand and truly repent?

If we look at Derek Chauvin through the eyes of wisdom, we see all the non-Derek Chauvin elements that make up who he is, like white supremacy, and the violent, racist history of policing in the United States among many other factors. We are a part of him, and he is a part of us. Just as we are all a part of George Floyd, and he is a part of us. We can all learn from the profound inclusiveness of the modern-day abolition movement, which envisions ways to stop systemic harm and uproot the dangerous beliefs at the root of hatred while at the same time encouraging everyone's flourishing through restoration, healing, and transformation rather than punishment and retaliation. As Mariame Kaba writes in *We Do This 'til We Free Us: Abolitionist Organizing and Transforming Justice,* "abolition is a vision of a restructured society where we have everything we need: food, shelter, education, health, art, beauty, clean water, and more things that are foundational to our personal and community safety."[13]

We can bring these radiant and powerful attitudes of equanimity and inclusiveness to our own difficulty or moment of transition. They keep us balanced, so although we rock this way and that like the Weeble, eventually we come back to our center. There are classical phrases for cultivating equanimity and inclusiveness that can help us in meditation. I invite you to try them out in the practice that follows.

MEDITATION

Begin by taking a few moments to feel your breathing, to feel your body. Allow yourself to open and settle, right here, right now …

Now visualize yourself in a large, open clearing or field, with grass, trees in the distance, and a big sky above. Allow yourself to open and settle in this spacious, calm place.

As you sit in this field, bring to mind a situation that's causing you some distress. Feel your body as you contemplate the situation. Maybe a decision you have to make, or a hard conversation you have to have with someone, or a struggle in some area of your life.

Now let your challenge, your question, something that is breaking your heart in the world, your moment of transition come and be with you in the field. Maybe it takes some kind of form like a shape, a color, a living being, or maybe it's a feeling, a sound, a scent. Whatever it is, let it be there, right next to you and try to get a felt sense for it. Now see a line on the ground that forms a circle around you both. The circle's diameter is just a few meters or yards across, so you and your question or difficulty are in a close space. Notice how this feels in your body.

Offer yourself these wishes:

> *May I open to this moment, just as it is*
> *May my heart be at ease with the conditions of*
> *my life*

Repeat each phrase a few times softly.

· · ·

Now see the circle growing bigger, ten yards in diameter. What is that like for you to experience more space around you and your difficulty? How do you feel? What happens in your body?

Practice with the equanimity phrase:

> *As much as I would like things to be different,*
> *things are the way they are in this moment*

. . .

And now the circle grows larger to twenty or thirty yards in diameter. How do you respond? How do you feel?

Continue to drop in the equanimity reflections:

> *May I open to the flow of joys and sorrows with*
> *understanding and equanimity*

. . .

Now the circle grows as large as the whole field, and there is so much space.

You can choose to go anywhere, have any relationship you wish to. It's your question. *Where do you wish to be in the field?* Let yourself go there. *Where is your question or difficulty in relation to you?* Notice how your choice feels in your body. Breathe with it. Allow whatever is here to be as it is.

If the phrases are helpful you can continue to use them, otherwise you can let them go:

> *May I open to this moment just as it is*
> *May my heart be at ease with the conditions*
> *of my life*

Now let yourself sit in the middle of the field

again. Your question or difficulty can be near or far away. Together enjoy watching the sun as it sets over the treetops and give yourself over to the beauty of this moment. See if in some way you can touch that all is well, even with your difficulty and question still there, not yet resolved. You must of course maintain your strength, your clarity, your purpose to resolve it, but you do not need to waste your energy in frustration, fear, and anxiety about it. Breathe in the beauty, the serenity of the moment.

May I open to this moment, just as it is

Now gently return to your body in the present moment, bring slow movements to your hands and feet, and take your time to open your eyes.

And when I rise, let me rise
Like a bird, joyfully
And when I fall, let me fall
Like a leaf, gracefully
Without regret

—Plum Village song

In Daily Life

We can bring the insight of equanimity into daily life by seeing the way others are us and we are them. A powerful practice as you move throughout your day is to notice the people, animals, plants, situations in your life and silently remind yourself, "This is me." When see a flower or a tree, "This is also me." When you encounter a person, "They are also me. I am also them."

ooooo

In this eighth chapter, we have explored the practice of equanimity and letting go to better meet times of challenge.

JOURNALING EXERCISE

How might the practice of equanimity and inclusiveness support you in the challenge or change you currently face?

By helping me to keep an open mind so I can move to the next rung of the ladder

By helping me to relax and not hold on so tightly to the outcome I desire

By helping me to see more sides of the situation and feel more space inside

By helping me accept what is and let go of fighting and resistance.

If any of these possible responses resonate with you, you could journal a few sentences about them and how you might practice them in the midst of your particular challenge or time of transition.

Chapter 9

NURTURING THE GOOD

> At some point in life, the world's beauty becomes enough.
>
> —Toni Morrison

> In the midst of winter, I finally learned that there was, within me, an invincible summer.
>
> —Albert Camus

We may believe that in order to be happy our suffering has to disappear completely. That they can't coexist. In my experience, even though I may be struggling in a time of transition or adversity, I can still be in touch with what is wholesome and good in me and around me. In fact, this is the moment I need it the most! Nurturing the good is crucial to our well-being and resilience in the face of change and tumult.

In Chapter 5, we spoke about taking care of the seeds in our store consciousness. Whatever we water in our daily life grows. The more we nurture the wholesome seeds, the stronger they become and the more resourced we will be when the storms of life hit.

And when we nurture the wholesome seeds, the unwholesome ones shrink all by themselves, without us having to do anything directly to weaken them, because we are giving more airtime to the seeds we want to manifest. Also, when a wholesome seed sprouts up, it stimulates other beautiful, wholesome seeds in our consciousness as well, making all of them stronger and more robust.

Gratitude is a very powerful way to nurture the good. Scholar and activist Joanna Macy says it's important to be grateful for things when they are going well, of course. But it's even more important to practice gratitude when things are not going well, when they aren't going according to our expectations. Gratitude helps us to keep our balance in those difficult situations. It calms our frantic minds and supports us to stay attentive to the possibilities that are still there. When I'm in a low mood, if I can remember to reflect on what I am grateful for, right away I experience more space inside. My heavy mood may not shift completely, but it begins to lift.

A few years ago, my maternal cousin's three daughters came to visit me and we spent two weeks together. They were eight, ten, and twelve years old at the time. I shared with them my practice of recalling something I was grateful for before eating and we got into the habit of doing that together at meals. At the end of our visit, we all took the train to attend a family reunion. It was a long train ride. By then we all felt tired, irritable, and a bit raggedy around the edges. I was sitting next to the ten-year-old, who was upset at her older sister for not sharing her phone. She was pouting and fuming. I asked her in a friendly way if she wanted to try an exercise with me to see if it would make her feel better. She agreed. I asked her to think of her mom and something she appreciated in her mom. She was quickly able to identify something. Then I asked about her grandmother, her younger sister, and her older sister (the very one who she was angry at), and she was able to find things she appreciated in each of them. I also asked what she appreciated in herself, and she brightened as she shared all this with me. I asked her how she felt after doing this, and she reported, "Much better." I suggested she could do this anytime she was upset. She said she'd try.

The next day the whole family had gathered at my father's house. We had prepared a delicious brunch and we were all hungry to enjoy it. The three girls appeared and said, "Wait! Before we eat, we have a game we want everyone to play." So, we waited, and they put a little piece of paper in front of everyone's plate. They then explained that it contained the name of someone else at the table, and we were going to go around the table and each share something we appreciated about the person whose name we'd been given. Everyone was taken by surprise because we'd never done this before. As we went around the circle, hearts opened, and smiles appeared. It was quite a holy moment.

Meister Eckhart, the thirteenth-century Dominican

friar and mystic, writes, "If the only prayer you ever say in your entire life is 'thank you' it will be enough."

Another time, I was offering a retreat for young people in Berlin and the following weekend I was to offer a retreat for artists. There was a young man attending the first retreat who also planned to attend the second one. He had just broken up with his partner of several years and was heartbroken and anguished. In the retreat I spoke about five practices we can do each day that are scientifically proven to increase happiness, compiled by Shawn Achor. They are what I call the Five Happinesses:

1. Meditate or pray.

2. Exercise.

3. Be aware of three new things we are grateful for.

4. Do a random or conscious act of kindness.

5. Journal about a happy moment from the day.[14]

At the first retreat, the young man committed to doing these five things each day. In the following retreat the next weekend he reported that even though he had come to Berlin in real despair, these five practices worked, and he was able to touch joy even in the midst of his pain.

There are research articles documenting the effects of gratitude on our health—it lowers blood pressure, improves sleep, strengthens immunity, and also supports us to have less conflict and more satisfaction in our relationships at home and at work. This makes us much stronger in trying times.

Practicing mindfulness, we can learn to give rise to contentment and peace at any moment, even really hard moments. The Buddha said happiness is available right in the present moment. That means right now! We can open our awareness to recognize the conditions for happiness that already exist. We don't need to go looking somewhere else, or in the past or future.

Thay often taught that we should live our life in such a way that we create a beautiful past. Once as a nun, I was traveling with a sister and two brothers to South Africa and Botswana to lead retreats. We had a few hours' wait in Johannesburg before our next flight, so we decided to have a meeting. One of the monks with us was of Vietnamese ancestry and he was quite a tea master. Before we began planning our various events, he wanted to serve us tea. So, he pulled out his fragile clay teapot, four glass tea cups, a thermos, and loose-leaf tea—all of which seemed to me very impractical to bring on such a long journey. He had filled his thermos with boiling water, with which he first washed the tea, then warmed up all the glasses with the hot water. Finally, he steeped the tea and poured us each a small glass. It was fragrant and delicious. This special ritual made all of us slow down and savor the moment. We moved from being somewhat harried about our work to enjoying each other, laughing, and relaxing as we sipped our tea.

He continued to serve us in this beautiful, mindful

way before every meeting we had on the trip. And we would enjoy our pause, our time to connect and just be. It always brought us closer and made our work together smoother and easier.

At the end of the trip, we finally had a day to just play. Our friends took us on a hike through the forest to a waterfall. It was beautiful! We swam across the forest pool as we wanted to climb up the waterfall on the other side. I noticed this brother was swimming with only one hand while he held his bag on his head with the other hand. I couldn't imagine why. We swam across and made our way up the huge boulders, about a fifty-foot climb, right to the top of the waterfall. We sat down on the large rock where the water began its descent, and we could see all around. And suddenly, out came the clay teapot, the glass teacups, the tea, and a thermos of boiling hot water! I was amazed! I felt so honored! It was like being royalty, being served tea in such a magnificent place. Remembering this moment always brings a smile to my face.

Even in times of hardship and transition, we can look for ways to bring joy and delight to ourselves and others in the present so that we create a beautiful past. We can remember what we are grateful for, and even in the midst of great trouble, we can find what is not going wrong.

MEDITATION

Nurturing the Good

Begin by settling into the body. Feel the breath, notice the environment, be aware of sounds, and connect with sensations in the body. Open to what's here in the body and mind, with acceptance and kindness.

If there is some sorrow, frustration, or difficulty you are experiencing in your body or your mind, allow it space to be here. Honor it and tend to it with friendliness. Breathe with it. Acknowledge it without pushing it away.

. . .

As you give it time and space, also, gently see if you can open to be aware of what is *not* going wrong. Notice what is happening even in the midst of this difficulty or pain that is going well, either in your body or mind. Feel into how both these things can coexist, the difficulty and the awareness of what is okay, what is good.

. . .

Now I invite you to appreciate yourself for your practice and the many ways that you are open to learn and grow. Something in you is energetic and motivated to grow and deepen; it cares about your own inner life, your own happiness. Feel the goodness of this impulse in you that brought you to practice in the first place. A kind of faith in yourself and your own inherent goodness. Feel it in your body. Notice its qualities and characteristics, this strength of mind/heart. Open to it, let it grow in you. Anchor it in a part of your body that resonates with this. And notice if there's a part of you that is more comfortable taking it for granted and that wants to focus on the parts of you that need to be "improved." Notice if there's resistance to allowing in the good. And if there is, see if you can give it space to shine just now.

. . .

Let yourself bring to mind other things you feel grateful for. How your body is still functioning right now, your heart still beating, your lungs expanding and retracting, your skin protecting your flesh.

Let yourself connect with gratitude for the presence of beloved people or pets in your life, or someone who has been supportive of you in the past. Connect with the ways they were present for you and how they made a difference in your life.

Reflect also on ways you have been supportive of others and let yourself feel gratitude for that, your own kindness, compassion, friendship to others. Feel how you made a difference to others and how this is significant.

. . .

Now let yourself open to gratitude for the world around you, the Earth that is supporting you right now, the sun that shows up each day, the air that sustains all life, water, the stars, the oceans. Feel the gift of life that is pulsing through your veins now and let yourself feel thankful for it. Feel the gift of life that surrounds you every moment, everywhere you go.

Feel this gratitude in your body. Let yourself be nurtured, strengthened by it.

And notice if there are any ideas arising about how you might create a beautiful past today or soon, for yourself and those you care about.

In Daily Life

You can practice the Five Happinesses each day, making space for meditation, exercise, recalling gratitude, a random act of kindness, or journaling a happy moment. For instance, you could invite someone to be your gratitude buddy and every day or every week, text each other what you are grateful for. I know a teacher who started doing this with a group of friends and they are still going strong some seven years later. Or reflect on a few things you are grateful for before you eat. It can also be wonderful to make it a practice to write an email or a note of appreciation to someone in your family or community every day for a week or two and notice how this affects you.

ooooo

In this ninth chapter, we have explored nurturing the good and the power of gratitude, especially in difficult times.

JOURNALING EXERCISE

Which of the following evidence-based ways to generate happiness and well-being is most realistic or appealing for you to incorporate into your daily life?

Meditation or prayer

Exercise

Reflecting on gratitude

Random acts of kindness

Journaling a happy moment

Why?

How might you grow your seeds of happiness and joy?

Chapter 10

WE WERE MADE FOR THESE TIMES

My friends, do not lose heart. We were made for these times. I have heard from so many recently who are deeply and properly bewildered.... Ours is a time of almost daily astonishment and often righteous rage over the latest degradations of what matters most....

You are right in your assessments.... Yet, I urge you, ask you, gentle you, to please not spend your spirit dry by bewailing these difficult times. Especially do not lose hope. Most particularly because, the fact is that we were made for these times. Yes. For years, we have been learning, practicing, been in training for and just waiting to meet on this exact plain of engagement.

—Clarissa Pinkola Estés
"Letter to a Young Activist
During Troubled Times"

When I was a teenager, I read numerous memoirs and novels about Civil Rights Movement activists and their courageous and intelligent organizing, putting their lives at risk and their families in danger to help transform our society. I remember passionately wishing I had been born in those times so that I could help change history the way they did.

The tremendous challenges humanity is now faced with are unlike any confronted by previous generations. Scientists on the Intergovernmental Panel on Climate Change have found that we have until 2030, less than a decade, to reduce carbon dioxide and other greenhouse gas emissions by 45 percent if our planet is to remain habitable. Interwoven with the koan of being good stewards of the only planet we have are the challenges of unraveling white supremacy and racial capitalism, toxic patriarchy, poverty on a global scale, homophobia, xenophobia, and the greed, hatred, and delusion at their roots. It is clear to me now that there is no other time I should have been born into. While the basic freedoms many enjoy today are due to the enormous sacrifices of the many young people of the Civil Rights Movement, I believe we are each called to continue their work in new ways to bring about even deeper freedom and greater awakening so that we can truly live harmoniously and altruistically with each other, our world, and all its species.

. . .

When I was in the process of deciding to leave monastic life, I was terrified. I had no idea what would come next, and I was giving up security, love, and belonging for a totally unknown future with absolutely no guarantees. Yet I knew I had to take the leap and leave the safety of my life to see what would await me. It was the first time in my life I was making a decision that was not supported by most of the people I loved and respected. But as I listened to my own intuition, my inner voice, I learned that I could trust it.

As soon as I made that first small, tentative step into the unknown, it was as if the earth rose up to meet my foot and supported me. One invitation to teach led to another and I was able to slowly begin to support myself and connect with communities that welcomed me, in all my awkwardness of moving out of one identity but not yet fully something else.

Each step gave me more faith and trust that I could do this. Life was calling to me to keep going and it continued to support me at every turn, even if I couldn't have seen quite how, just one or two steps back. I just kept going and sure enough there was a way for me. By walking, one makes the road," as the poet Antonio Machado writes.

For nearly twenty years I had been singing a song our community sang often, "Here Is the Pure Land." It includes this line: "The Sangha body is everywhere; my true home is right here." The "Sangha body" means the community of those practicing the path of awareness and compassion. Only when I left the monastery and was received and nourished by spiritual community after spiritual community in many parts of the world did I realize the deeper meaning of this line in the song. As a nun I believed the monastic community was the only place I could truly practice deeply, and part of my terror of leaving was the fear that I would lose my practice without the twenty-four-hour-a-day support

WE WERE MADE FOR THESE TIMES

of a residential monastic community. But as I traveled and led retreats and events on my own for the first time, I experienced more and more clearly lay communities that were extremely dedicated and put incredible energy into nourishing their local groups with mindfulness.

On previous teaching trips, I had always travelled with another nun. Now that I was alone with the communities I was visiting, we were more vulnerable with each other. The barrier between monastics and laypeople began to come down, and I experienced how held and supported I was by the Sangha body that was truly everywhere. And how my true home is right here, not only in the monastery around other monastics, but also in the middle of daily life in a busy city surrounded by all kinds of people. My true home is anywhere there is practice, anywhere I am showing up fully present to connect and be with others. I began to touch and understand that I already had everything I needed.

Understanding on this deeper level that my true home is right here wherever I am also leaves me full of gratitude and reverence for the precious contribution that the monastics and the monasteries make to our world, without which I wouldn't be who I am. They have a unique role in helping to preserve the heart of many of our traditions. I continue to stay connected to the monastic Sangha and be deeply nourished by these noble practitioners.

What can be so stressful in moments of change or challenge is feeling unprepared, caught off-guard, somehow out of control. But if we shift our perspective right in the midst of this falling and losing control, we can maintain our balance *inside of us* and touch the many resources we *already have* to meet the unexpected. We must learn to do this both as individuals and as a collective. The elders of the Hopi Nation in Oraibi, Arizona, offered this timely wisdom:

> ... There is a river flowing now very fast. It is so great and swift that there are those who will be afraid. They will try to hold on to the shore. They will feel they are torn apart and will suffer greatly. Know the river has its destination. The elders say we must let go of the shore, push off into the middle of the river, keep our eyes open, and our heads above water. And I say, see who is in there with you and celebrate. At this time in history, we are to take nothing personally, least of all ourselves. For the moment that we do, our spiritual growth and journey comes to a halt.
>
> The time for the lone wolf is over. Gather yourselves! Banish the word struggle from your attitude and your vocabulary. All that we do now must be done in a sacred manner and in celebration.

We are the ones we've been waiting for.[15]

Though the river is moving very fast, it has its destination; we can trust this. We don't need to know the destination. We do need to keep our eyes open and see who is with us and celebrate. Because we are the ones we've been waiting for.

Whatever travails or transitions you are facing in this moment, please remember: we were made for these times. Whenever we come home to this moment, whenever we engage in mindfulness practices like the ones we have learned in this book, this is preparing us, in every breath, in every step, to meet the suffering and challenges of this moment.

In this last meditation we will utilize the power of visualization. When we visualize ourselves doing something, the brain and the body experience it as if we have *actually done* it in real life. Then when we do that activity or are in the real situation, our body and mind are much more prepared. Athletes and dancers regularly use this practice to help them hone their skill. As meditators we can do it, too!

MEDITATION

Settling now into a comfortable position. Feeling your body settling and arriving. Connect with the breath and let yourself enjoy a deep inhale and a long, slow exhale. Rest here, connecting to yourself and the earth.

Now see yourself continuing to move through your challenge or transition until you reach the other side of it. See how you will look and feel when the storm has settled, confident, at peace. Now I'll guide you in a detailed way, to visualize yourself using the tools of this book to meet whatever challenges, fears, or confusion may arise.

Picture yourself coming home to your body and mind, taking good care of this moment, as the best way to take care of the future. See yourself getting so good at it that it becomes a habit, and your finding yourself in a place where you are more often than not at home in yourself. What does that feel like in your body?

Imagine yourself resting back and trusting the unknown, as you let the big questions or problems you face rest like a seed in the soil of your mind, maturing in their own time. You have that patience, that calm. Feel it growing in you day by day.

And you are growing this big heart capable of accepting what is, namely suffering, so that you don't make it worse by resisting it. What is that like, to know you can accept whatever comes your way? To not be afraid? Touch that reality inside you now.

See yourself confidently weathering the storms by coming down to the trunk of your tree to breathe deeply in your belly and walk or move with kind attention to each step or movement. And you discover and apply new practices as you need them as well. Experience confidence now, down in your bones, knowing you have many tools you can rely on to see you through whenever you need them.

As you breathe in and out, visualize yourself mindfully and wisely caring for disturbing emotions with compassion, becoming more and more free of unhelpful patterns, until these emotions have less and less of a hold on you. How does your face look in such a state of skillfully working with your strong emotions? How does your body feel? Let yourself feel this now.

Picture yourself aware of impermanence from moment to moment, allowing the Five Remembrances to remind you to meet the inevitability of loss and separation with an open heart and a clear mind.

And see yourself remaining unmoved by the tumult of the eight worldly winds, swayed by neither praise nor blame, remaining in the eye of the wheel, and going beneath the surface of the waves to touch the peace and vastness of water. How does it feel to move through the world when you understand you are not a separate self, but full of everything? Notice the clarity and the peace this brings.

And see yourself with a calm smile on your face as you master that grandmotherly love, of equanimity and inclusiveness that doesn't attach or cling. Your inner Weeble always finds its way back to center. How does it feel to know you can trust yourself, to know you can always find a way to be more and more at ease with the conditions of your life?

And you are moving through your life able to harness the power of nurturing the good, skillfully calling up gratitude—especially when times are tough. You are skilled at creating moments of happiness for yourself and others. See it concretely now. What does that look and feel like? Who are you bringing joy to? Let your body experience that now.

And then see that everything you have experienced in your life has led you to this moment, which is exactly where you need to be. You were made for these times, to meet this moment as it is, whatever it brings. You have everything you need to do that. Feel that confidence, that ease.

Take a few minutes to be in this place on the other side of your difficulty as fully and as viscerally as you can.

As we are facing not only individual challenges and transitions, but also collective ones, take a moment now to connect with one aspect of our current collective crises that is particularly important or resonant for you. Maybe it's connected to how humans are harming the Earth, or oppressing each other; maybe it's related to perpetual wars or the suffering of refugees and immigrants, or systemic racism, or crushing poverty and debt. Feel the weightiness of whichever issue or crisis you have chosen.

And now, just as we did for the personal challenge, see in your mind's eye what it would mean for the collective to address this difficulty with wisdom. Visualize what real freedom, justice, and compassion would look and feel like if this crisis were resolved, deeply understood, and no longer perpetuated. Reparations made, repentance offered on a global scale, wealth equitably shared, reliable structures set up that would offer true safety, lasting peace, and profound healing for all humans, all species, and the Earth herself.

Open to the possibility that this could exist and notice how it feels in your body. And now imagine that you could contribute to this.

We were made for these times … in every way.

. . .

Dear friend, let's continue this practice, only now using phrases to deepen this intention for ourselves to be well in this time of change and challenge. If you'd like, you can close your eyes, place a hand over your heart, and send yourself these good wishes:

> *May I be well. May I have all that I need to go through these difficulties. May I trust and let go. May I dwell in my true home.*

Again, see this being so in your mind's eye.

It is also important to remember that you are not alone in what you are going through. Bring to mind people you know who are also encountering times of challenge and transition. Maybe friends or family, other people who are also reading this book with you, and now anyone anywhere who may be struggling. Know we are all connected. While the circumstances may be different, the experiences of confusion, fear, anger, and sadness are common to all of us.

Allow your heart to open in compassion as you include them in your wishes as well.

> *May you be well. May you have all that you need to go through the difficulties you are facing. May you trust and let go. May you rest in your true home.*

Feel the sincere wish for anyone and everyone facing a time of challenge to be able to find and dwell in their true home. See it being so.

> *May I be happy,*
> *May I be free from pain and suffering,*
> *May I live with peace and well-being,*
> *and may I be free.*
> *May (you, we, all beings) be happy...*
> *May (you, we, all) be free from pain and suffering,*
> *May (you, we, all) live with peace and well-being,*
> *and may (you, we, all) be free.*
>
> —"Loving Kindness,"
> song from Sister Hai An,
> Melina Bondy

In Daily Life

When you find yourself in difficulty in daily life, remember your connection to others. Others who are supporting you and also others who are going through challenging times like you are. Include them in your awareness and send gratitude for those that strengthen you, and wish those in difficulty all the support they need to go through what they are encountering. Let yourself feel solidarity with them in your common struggles.

Also, if you aren't already familiar, familiarize yourself with groups and movements that are making a difference in our world and actually helping a new reality come into being.

Each of us has affinity for varied aspects of our shared condition. For myself, my solidarity may come in the form of regular engagement or sending support to specific efforts like Project Drawdown, Black Lives Matter, Sunrise Movement, the prison industrial complex abolition movement, or the Poor People's Campaign. There are many others that are taking meaningful steps to heal our society and our relationship with our planet. If you are able, reflect on how you might engage with or be of support to these movements, perhaps with a small group of others in an action pod. Together, as we learn and engage, we can embody the truth that we were made for these times.

JOURNALING EXERCISE

Having completed this book, what best describes where you are now in relation to the challenge or transition you are facing?

I have concrete tools I am eager to use.

I am happier and more settled.

I am less fearful and anxious.

I am more confident in myself.

In what other ways are you holding your challenge or difficulty differently than when you started this book?

How do you experience in yourself that you were made for these times?

Where or how are you inspired to engage with situations that you care about in the world?

I have so appreciated the opportunity to go on this journey with you and hope it has been meaningful and helpful to you. I have faith and confidence in you and the wisdom in you that brought you to this book. I wish you ever-deepening freedom and realization as you move through whatever challenge or transition you are currently facing.

ACKNOWLEDGMENTS

In the Plum Village Buddhist tradition, at the beginning of formal ceremonies and to mark important moments of making vows and committing to shift our lives in a significant way, we honor four groups of people with a full bow, or prostration to the earth. These are our parents, teachers, friends, and all beings. I am using this framework to express my acknowledgments and thanks here.

I will always be grateful to my parents, both deeply spiritual seekers, who decided they were made for these times by choosing an interracial marriage in Chicago in 1970 and dedicating their lives to caring for those who suffer around the world. Thank you for nurturing the best in me. You are in every cell of my body and in every word in this book.

Everything I have shared here and my entire Dharma life exists because of my teachers—both monastic and lay. I bow in deep gratitude to Thich Nhat Hanh, my root teacher, who quickened the transformation of my suffering through his compassion and strengthened my faith in my own capacity to awaken with his happiness and confidence in me. Sister Chan Không, Sister Chan Duc (Sr. Annabel) and Sister Dieu Nghiem (Sr. Jina) have been steady, loving mentors and powerful models of bodhicitta in action, providing a rich foundation for my monastic life through their teaching and practice. I am deeply grateful to Joseph Goldstein, Carol Wilson, and the whole IMS community who introduced me to the Vipassana lineage and its unique gifts. Thank you so much for not only the gift of Dharma, but also your deeply generous material support. I extend heartfelt gratitude to Tara Brach and everyone at the Insight Meditation Community of Washington (IMCW) who supported me in my first years of teaching in Washington DC. I offer the deepest respect and love to Larry Yang, Gina Sharpe, and Kate Lila Wheeler, as well as Rachel Bagby, who gave your all to love us into our fullness and open the doors wide to each of us in the Spirit Rock Teacher Training, and to Jack Kornfield who believed in us all. I am also fortunate to have Thanissara and Kittisaro as immensely inspiring mentors. I have been profoundly impacted by the InterPlay community, founded by Cynthia Winton-Henry and Phil Porter, who playfully and respectfully opened new windows in my mind and invited me more deeply into my body. And Stephanie, I cannot thank you enough. I have received the immeasurable in your loving presence.

I deeply thank all my elder and younger monastic siblings, a true Sangha body that guided, protected, and nourished me like nothing else in my life before or since. Thank you for teaching me to be a happy nun and for letting me go. My clearness committee was a timely blessing and catalyst: Bettina Romhardt, Michael May, Barbara Casey, Sumi Kim, Elizabeth Dearborn and Robyn Sheldon, thank you for your friendship and love. I am grateful to my brother, Adam, and sister, Traci, for your humor, wisdom, listening, and love during the major transitions and the warm welcome back to lay life.

I also thank whose who offered precious support and friendship as I started over: Mitchell Ratner and Ann-Mari Gemmill, Marisela Gomez, Richard Brady, Lyn Fine, John Bell, Peggy and Larry Ward, Eileen Kiera, Valerie Brown, Ven. Satima, Annabelle Zinser, Sister Bi Nghiem, Sister Peace, Sister True Vow, Adrianna Rocco, Anita Constantini, Emanuela Sandini, Letizia and Stefano Carboni, Ivo Scheppers and Annette Schramm, Verena Böttcher, Renuka Bhakta, Yvonne Fuchs, Beth Sanchez, Jeanine Cogan, Sharron Swain, Melina Bondy, John Salunga, Dr. Vincent Harding, Tom Holmes and everyone at Gilchrist Retreat Center, Claire W., as well as the whole community at Schumacher College, especially Tim Crabtree, Satish Kumar and June Mitchell, and Sophy Banks.

I offer such gratitude for my DC beloveds for helping me create a new home: Julia Jarvis and the Monday Night Sangha, Annie Mahon and everyone at Circle Yoga and Opening Heart Mindfulness Community, La Sarmiento, Em Morrison, Kristin Barker, Lauren Taylor, Travis Spencer, Satyani McPherson, Dave Trachtenberg, Bruce Gill, Gretchen Rohr, Kate Amoss, Katrina Browne, and Cassie Meador. To all my Inward

Bound Mindfulness Education (iBme) colleagues and the young people I had a chance to practice with, you brought a powerful direction to my life, and lots of fun! Thank you. To my friends from Sri Lanka, your wisdom, gentleness, and fierce strength was a true lifeline. Thank you Sahan Dharmatilleke, Niluka Gunawardena, Dinusha Wickremasekera, Merhawi Teklebran and Abeba Petros, Kamani Jinadasa and the Wisdom Wednesdays crew. I also bow to each of my siblings in Spirit Rock Teacher Training, I love you all and carry you in me.

I also thank Natascha Bruckner for her thorough, thoughtful, and loving editing. I have enjoyed the journey of bringing this book into being because of Hisae Matsuda's skillfulness, warmth, and clarity as Parallax publisher. To the whole Parallax team: I know I am in good hands with you.

This book would not have come to be without my beloved partner, Adam, who first encouraged me to turn the course I had created into a book and patiently read through numerous versions. Thank you for nurturing me to blossom into the fullness that I am here to be.

I am grateful to all beings everywhere who make my life and this book possible.

NOTES

Opening epigraph

1. Amanda Gorman, *The Hill We Climb: An Inaugural Poem for the Country* (New York: Viking, 2021).

Preface

2. The title for this book *We Were Made for These Times* is inspired by the moving essay "Letter to a Young Activist During Troubled Times" with the subtitle "Do Not Lose Heart, We Were Made for These Times," © 2001, 2016 by Clarissa Pinkola Estés, http://clarissapinkolaestes.com.

Chapter 1: Coming Home

3. The ten-day course "We Were Made for These Times" is available on Insight Timer. Visit https://insighttimer.com/meditation-courses/course_we-were-made-for-these-times-10-lessons-in-moving-through-change-loss-and-disruption.

Chapter 2: Resting Back and Trusting the Unknown

4. Alan Watts, *The Wisdom of Insecurity* (New York: Vintage), 2011.

Chapter 3: Accepting What Is

5. Kittisaro, quoted in Leslee Goodman, "A Mindful Marriage," *The Sun Magazine*, January 2009, https://www.thesunmagazine.org/issues/397/a -mindful-marriage.

6. From Rainer Maria Rilke, "Let This Darkness Be a Bell Tower," *Sonnets to Orpheus* II, 29, in Anita Barrows and Joanna Macy, trans., *In Praise of Mortality: Selections from Rainer Maria Rilke's* Duino Elegies *and* Sonnets to Orpheus (Brattle-boro, VT: Echo Point Books, 2016).

Chapter 4: Weathering the Storm

7. Matthew Huston wrote a beautiful article about moving in a wheelchair in Plum Village Community of Engaged Buddhism, *The Mindfulness Bell*, vol. 35, Winter/Spring 2004, which can be read at https://www.mindfulnessbell.org/archive /tag/wheelchair.

Chapter 5: Caring for Strong Emotions

8. The Five Remembrances in the Plum Village

tradition can be found in many books, including Thich Nhat Hanh, *Chanting from the Heart* (Berkeley, CA: Parallax Press, 2006).

Chapter 7: Calmly Facing the Eight Worldly Winds

9. Matty Weingast, *The First Free Women: Poems Inspired by the Early Buddhist Nuns* (Boulder, CO: Shambhala Publications), 2020.

10. Thich Nhat Hanh, *Teachings on Love* (Berkeley, CA: Parallax Press, 2002).

11. Thomas Merton, *Conjectures of a Guilty Bystander* (New York: Crown Publishing, 2009), 155.

Chapter 8: Equanimity and Letting Go

12. Martin Luther King, "Loving Your Enemies" sermon delivered at Dexter Avenue Baptist Church, Montgomery, Alabama, November 17, 1957. Published in Clayborne Carson, ed., *A Knock at Midnight: Inspiration from the Great Sermons of Martin Luther King, Jr.* (New York: IPM/Warner Books), 1998.

13. Mariame Kaba, *We Do This 'Til We Free Us: Abolitionist Organizing and Transforming Justice* (Chicago: Haymarket Books), 2021.

Chapter 9: Nurturing the Good

14. Shawn Achor, "The Happiness Advantage: Linking Positive Brains to Performance," TEDxBloomington. YouTube, June 30, 2011. https://www.youtube.com/watch?v=GXy__kBVq1M.

Chapter 10: We Were Made for These Times

15. A Prophecy from the Hopi Elders spoken at Oraibi, Arizona, June 8, 2000, in Margaret Wheatley, *Perseverance* (San Francisco: Berrett-Koehler, 2010), iii.

ABOUT THE AUTHOR

Kaira Jewel Lingo is a Dharma teacher with a life-long interest in blending spirituality and meditation with social justice. Having grown up in an ecumenical Christian community where families practiced a new kind of monasticism and worked with the poor, at the age of twenty-five she entered a Buddhist monastery in the Plum Village tradition and spent fifteen years living as a nun under the guidance of Zen Master Thich Nhat Hanh. She received authorization to teach from Thich Nhat Hanh and became a Zen teacher in 2007. She is also a teacher in the Vipassana Insight lineage through Spirit Rock Meditation Center. Today she sees her work as a continuation of the Engaged Buddhism developed by Thich Nhat Hanh as well as the work of her parents, inspired by their stories and her father's work with Dr. Martin Luther King Jr. on desegregating the South.

In addition to writing *We Were Made for These Times*, she is also the editor of Thich Nhat Hanh's book *Planting Seeds: Practicing Mindfulness with Children*. She teaches and leads retreats internationally, provides spiritual mentoring, and interweaves art, play, nature, racial and Earth justice, and embodied mindfulness practice in her teaching. She especially feels called to share the Dharma with Black, Indigenous, and People of Color, as well as activists, educators, youth, artists, and families. Visit kairajewel.com to learn more.

RELATED TITLES FROM PARALLAX PRESS

America's Racial Karma: An Invitation to Heal by Larry Ward, PhD

Brothers in the Beloved Community: The Friendship of Thich Nhat Hanh and Martin Luther King Jr. by the Rt. Rev. Marc Andrus

The Eight Realizations of Great Beings: Waking Up to Who You Are by Brother Phap Hai

Healing Resistance: A Radically Different Response to Harm by Kazu Haga

Love Letter to the Earth by Thich Nhat Hanh

Love in Action: Writings on Nonviolent Social Change by Thich Nhat Hanh

Moments of Joy: The Poems of Sister Jina, Chan Dieu Nghiem by Sister Jina van Hengel.

True Virtue: The Journey of an English Buddhist Nun by Sister Annabel Laity.

World as Lover, World as Self: Courage for Global Justice and Planetary Awakening 30th Anniversary Edition by Joanna Macy

PARALLAX PRESS, a nonprofit publisher founded by Zen Master Thich Nhat Hanh, publishes books and media on the art of mindful living and Engaged Buddhism. We are committed to offering teachings that help transform suffering and injustice. Our aspiration is to contribute to collective insight and awakening, bringing about a more joyful, healthy, and compassionate society.

View our entire library at parallax.org.

THE MINDFULNESS BELL, a journal of the art of mindful living in the tradition of Thich Nhat Hanh, is published twice a year by our community. To subscribe or to see the worldwide directory of Sanghas, or local mindfulness groups, visit mindfulnessbell.org.